# CORPORATE IMAGES:

Photography and the
Du Pont Company
1865–1972

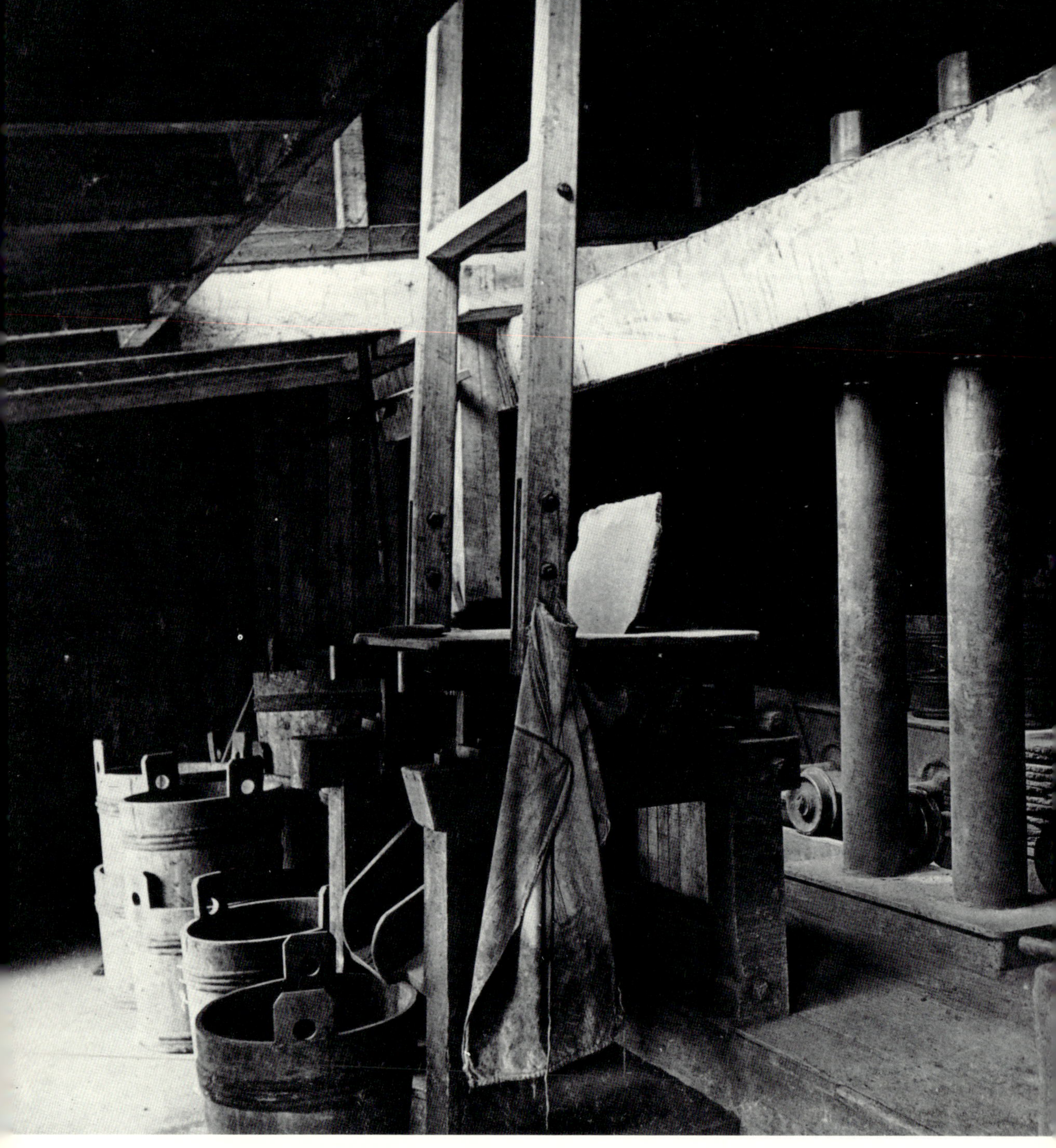

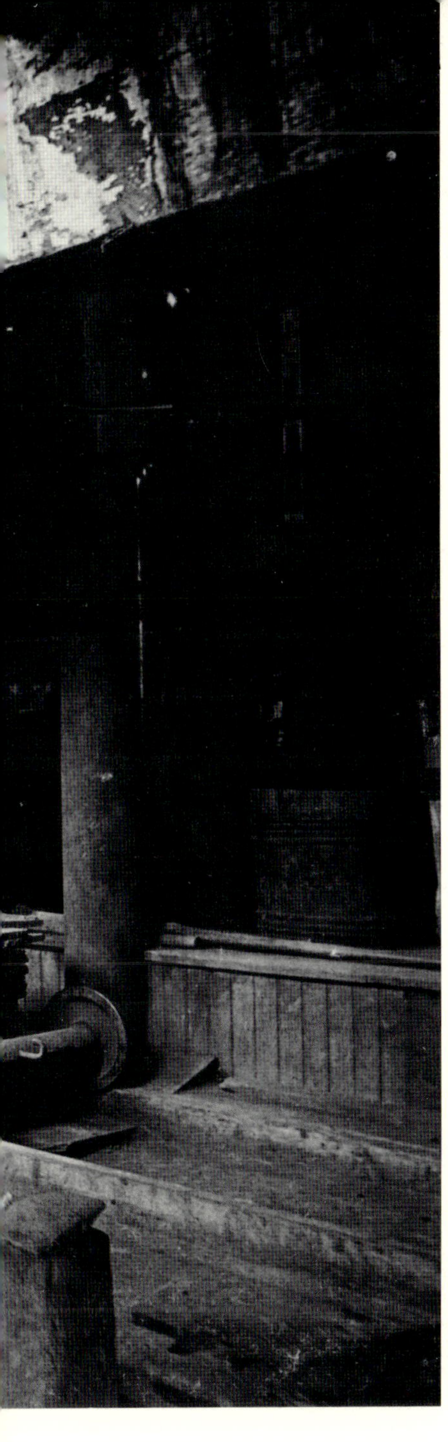

# CORPORATE IMAGES:

## Photography and the Du Pont Company 1865–1972

Jon M. Williams and Daniel T. Muir

HAGLEY MUSEUM AND LIBRARY

WILMINGTON, DELAWARE

A HAGLEY COLLECTIONS GUIDE

Cover: *Better Living* staff photographer Alex Henderson at work, reflected in a laboratory flask.

Frontispiece: Interior of a press mill in the powder yards photographed by Henry B. du Pont, c. 1895.

Overleaf: John A. Dick with Cirkut camera used for taking panoramic photographs.

Back cover: Equipment used in the manufacture of sulfuric acid at Du Pont's East Chicago, Indiana plant.

International Standard Book Number: 0-914650-24-6
© The Eleutherian Mills-Hagley Foundation
Printed in the United States of America

# CONTENTS

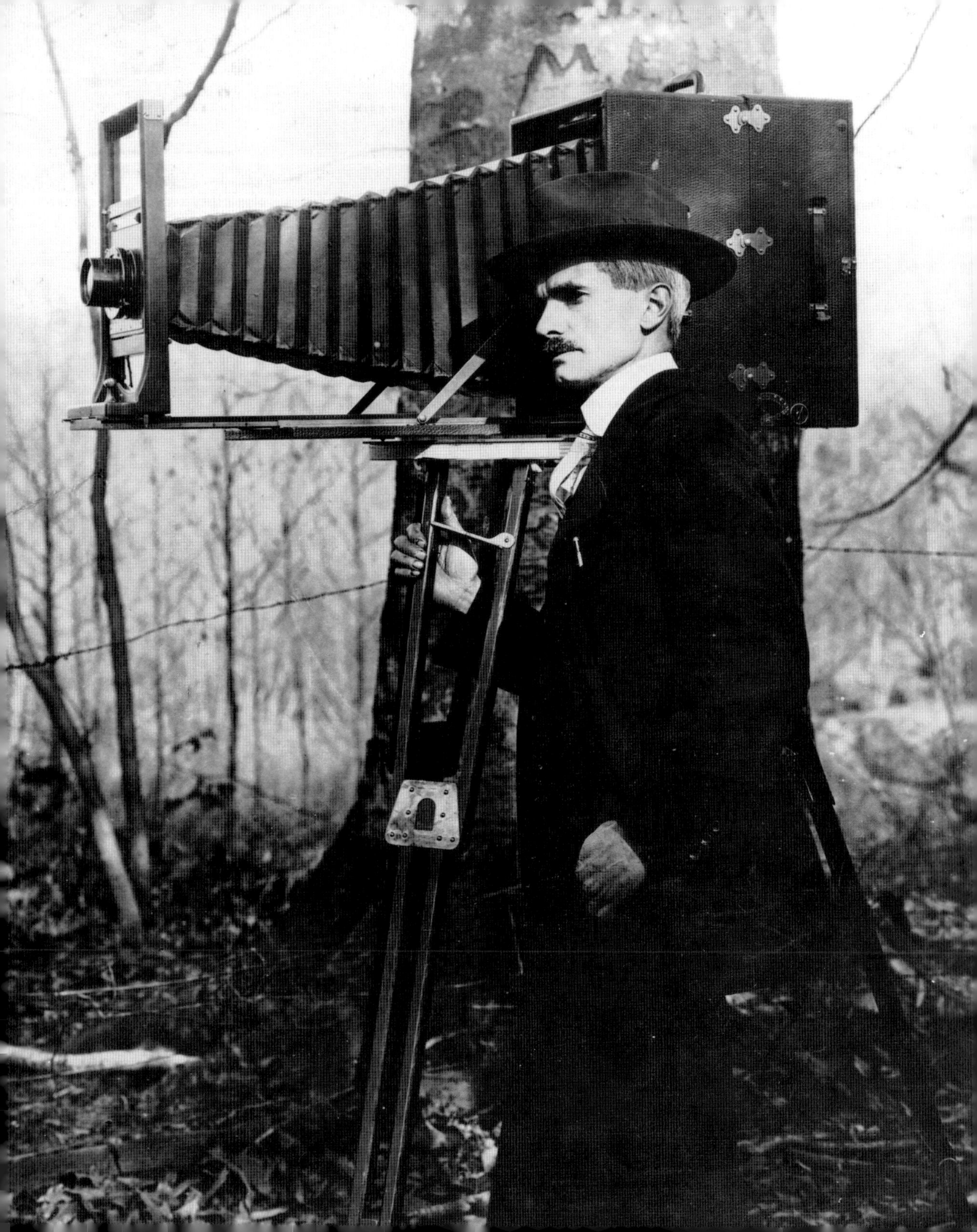

# PREFACE

This publication offers a sampling of one of Hagley's great pictorial collections—the photographs associated with the history of the Du Pont Company. Numbering some 350,000 items in 1984, Hagley's photographic collections are a national treasure in the area of business and technological history. The materials documented in this booklet account for fewer than one-quarter of all our historical images, but they are among our most significant groups of photographs, in part because of the superb associated manuscript and imprint records that we also hold. As historians and indeed all Americans explore the origins and evolution of our modern economy and society, graphic evidence such as these photographs will play a central role.

This is the latest in a series of publications designed to make potential researchers better informed about Hagley's collections, and to make easier the use of those materials. Many of our manuscript collections have already been described in publications by John Beverly Riggs, former Curator of Manuscripts: *A Guide to the Manuscripts in the Eleutherian Mills Historical Library: Accessions through the Year 1965* (1970) and the supplement covering the years 1966–1975 (1978). A small booklet entitled *Pictorial Collections* was published in 1974. We will soon be issuing *Pennsylvania Power and Light: A Guide to the Collections,* thereby improving scholarly access to one of the largest and most important collections we have acquired in recent years.

This publication appeared in connection with "Corporate Images," a temporary exhibit in the fall of 1984 at the Hagley Museum and Library. We hope in the years to come to publish more guides to our important collections of artifacts, manuscripts, pictorial materials, and imprints. Hagley's collections are a unique national resource, and through publications such as this one we intend to make Americans better aware of this important part of their heritage.

GLENN PORTER
DIRECTOR
HAGLEY MUSEUM AND LIBRARY

THE INDUSTRIAL PHOTOGRAPHS at the Hagley Museum and Library (estimated at 350,000 in 1984) are an integral part of our programs to collect, preserve, interpret and promote research in American business and technological history, particularly in our region. Major collections illustrate developments in many industries—iron and steel, leather, data processing, chemical, power generation, bridge construction, petroleum, shipbuilding, railroad and aviation. An illustrated brochure briefly describing many of the collections is available by writing to Hagley at P. O. Box 3630, Wilmington, DE 19807.

The Hagley Museum and Library is located on the site of the first Du Pont manufactory, established in 1802. Du Pont Company industrial records, including publications, manuscripts, artifacts, and illustrative materials, are a significant part of the research collections. Du Pont Company photography at Hagley is not one unified collection, but rather consists of many groups of images received over the past three decades.

The main body of this booklet is devoted to the historical development of photography within Du Pont, and to its uses as elucidated in the firm's manuscripts, publications, and pictorial collections at Hagley. It is limited to photography documented in Hagley's holdings, and does not include current photographic practices, paintings, or other forms of art work.

Any significant research in the collections must be done in person. The staff will respond to brief inquiries by correspondence, and we will advise potential researchers whether a visit to Hagley would be fruitful for a particular topic. Inquiries about the collections should be addressed to the Curator of Prints and Photographs at the above address. Send requests concerning printed or manuscript materials to the Research and Reference Librarian. Those interested in artifacts must contact the Curator of Collections. Research visits should be scheduled in advance, if possible, to ensure researchers the full benefit of our staff's knowledge of the collections.

# CORPORATE IMAGES:

Photography and the
Du Pont Company
1865–1972

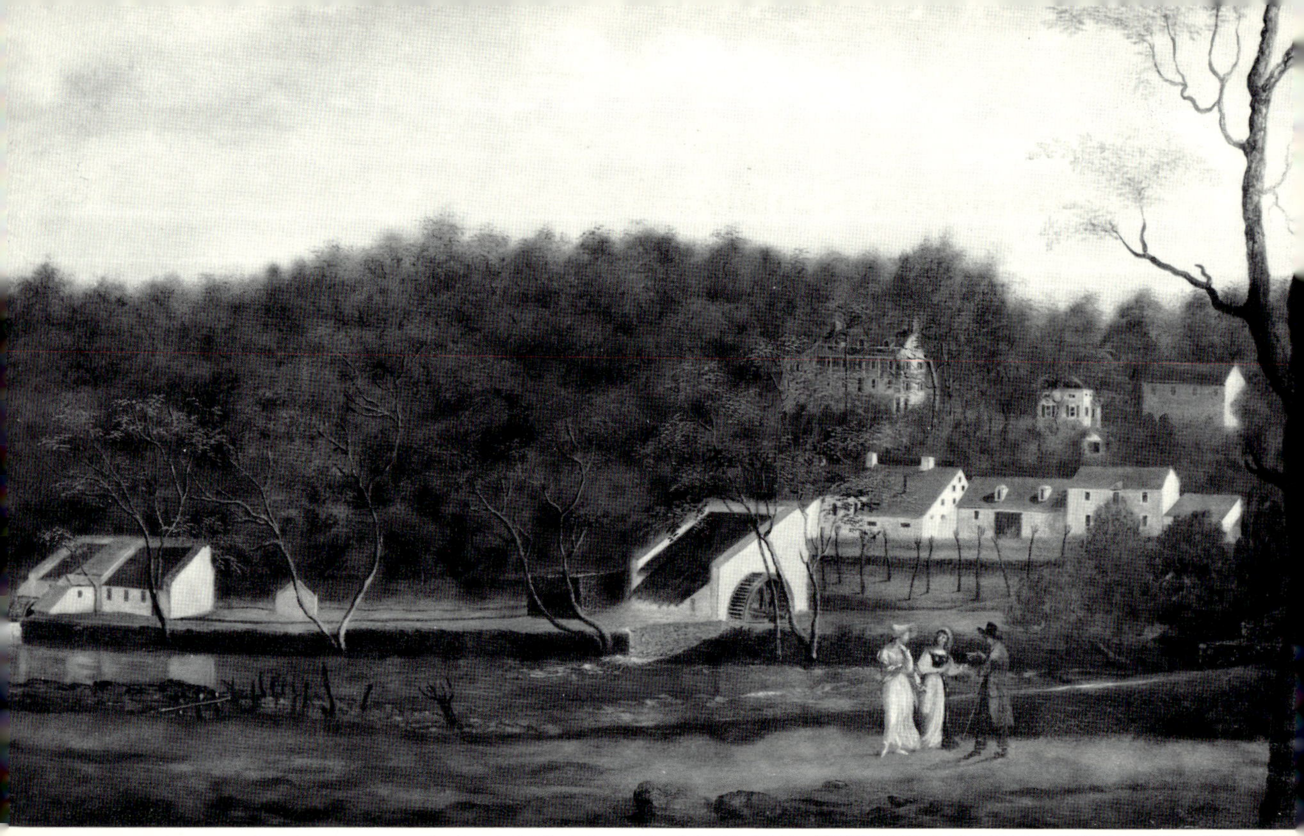

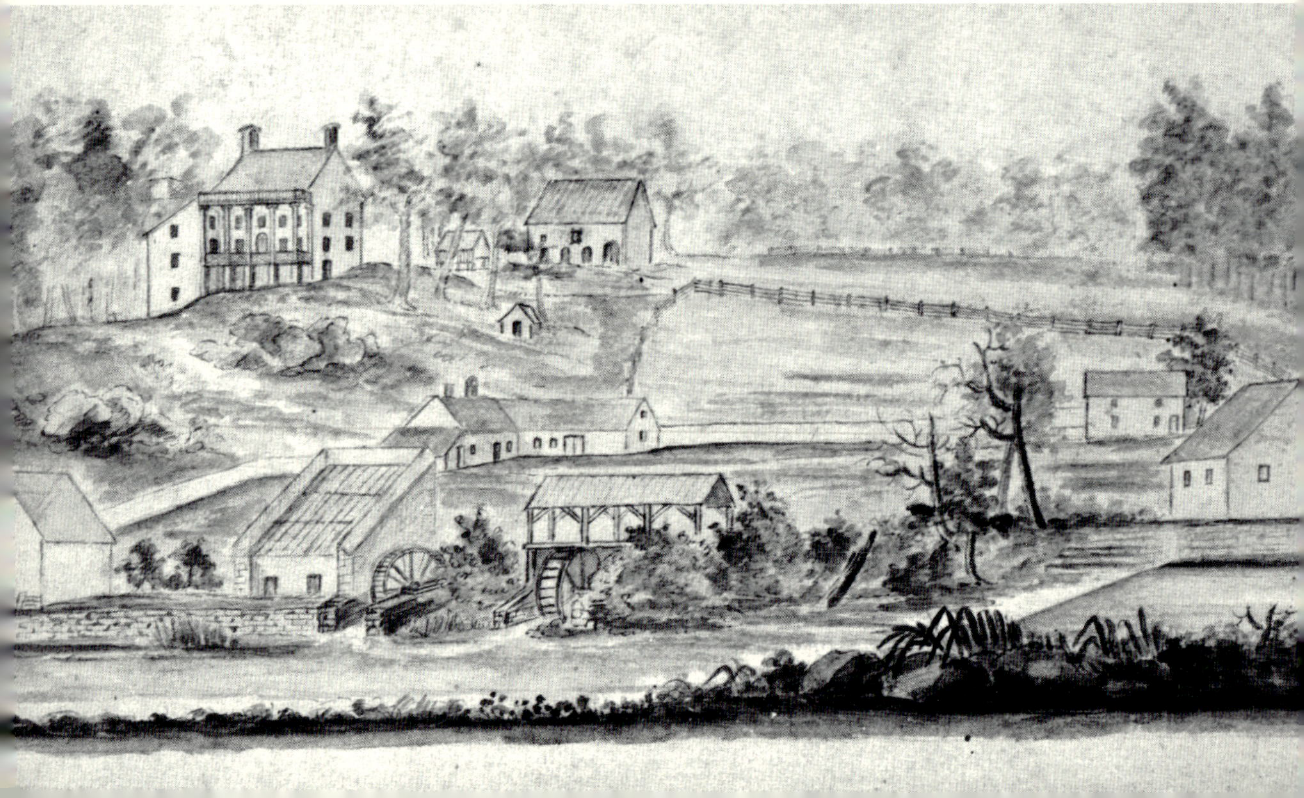

# A Tradition of Images

THE first known visual representation of the activities and properties of the Du Pont Company dates to 1806. The early years of the company were fraught with financial crises, and many times shareholders had to be convinced that the business was viable. We owe the earliest known picture of the company's operations to one of those crises. In 1806, Charles Dalmas, brother-in-law of Eleuthere Irénée du Pont, made a watercolor sketch of the Eleutherian Mills powder yard in order to show backers in France the extent of what they were backing. It was evidently felt that a picture, even a sketch, would be more reassuring than a verbal description. Although the picture did little to allay the fears of some of the stockholders, it was the forerunner of many to come, and is indicative of the important role that pictures, especially photographs, would play in the Du Pont Company throughout its history.

Founded on the Brandywine Creek in Delaware by E. I. du Pont in 1802 and producing black powder by 1804, the Du Pont powder mills[1] brought a more sophisticated technology and a larger scale to the explosives industry in America than had previously existed. This, coupled with the rapid growth of the new country, made possible a secure business niche for the firm. The company

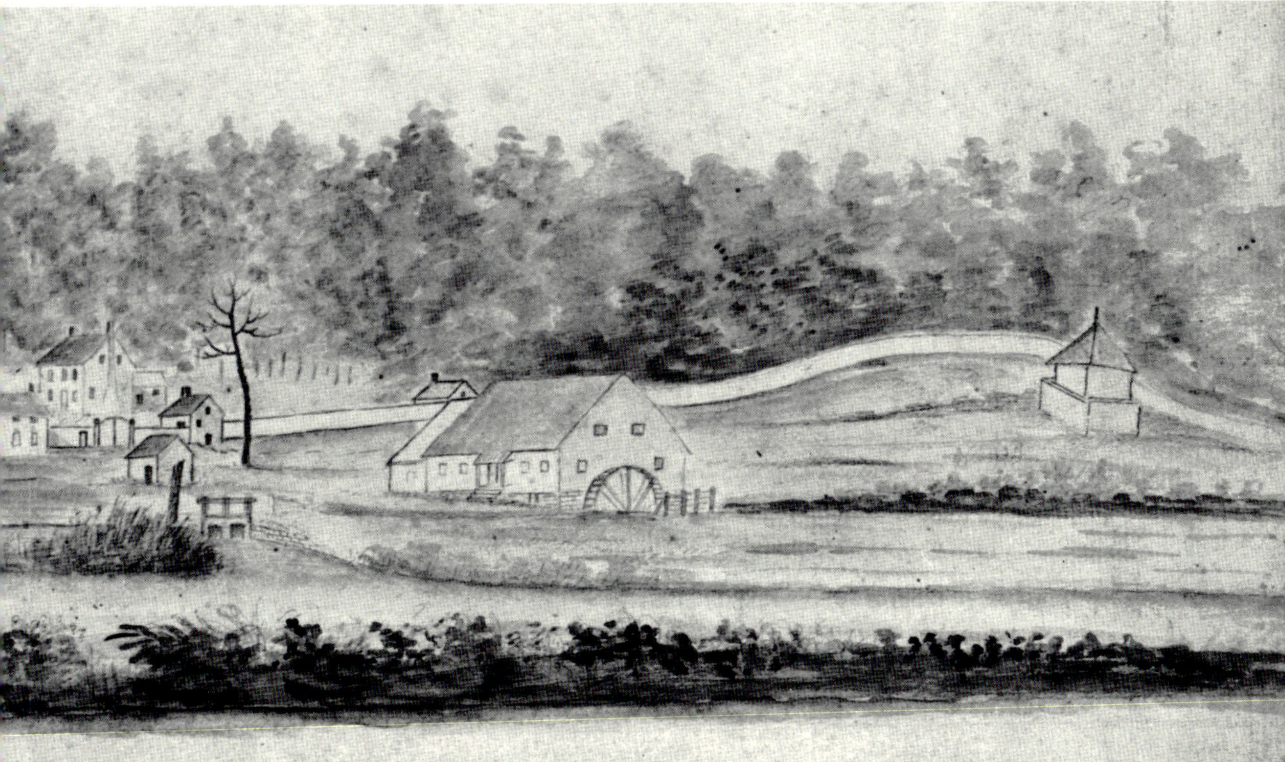

did not, however, enjoy a straightforward rise to bigness. The vagaries of the American economy, the anxieties of stockholders, and the nativist prejudices of the young country all had their effects upon the Du Pont Company's fortunes. Explosions and other technical difficulties played their part, too, in making life difficult on the Brandywine. But the company did grow, and eventually it prospered. Even in the pre-photographic period (prior to 1840), the activities of the firm were occasionally recorded in pictures.

The young nation attracted a great number of visitors in the early 1800s, many of them armed with sketch books and paintbrushes. French visitors especially were welcomed to the small community of French emigrés in Wilmington, and particularly to the Du Pont establishment on the Brandywine. The earliest of these visitors to leave behind a pictorial record was the Baronness Hyde de Neuville, who came in 1810 and drew a few pencil sketches of the powder buildings and the du Pont home. She was followed in the 1820s by Charles A. Lesueur and August Plée, both artists and naturalists. These men left behind rough sketches of the Brandywine area, often incompletely identified, but nevertheless valuable to historians.

One set of artists were not travelers but rather natives of the Brandywine area. One of the desirable "accomplishments" for young ladies of the period was a facility with a sketch pad and pencil, and E. I. du Pont's daughters were no different in this regard from any other young American ladies. They were all voracious sketchers, and they have left behind a legacy of multitudinous sketches that tell us a great deal about the Brandywine at the time. However, they were not trained observers of industrial processes and were probably seldom allowed into the dangerous powder yards, so the sketches tell us little about the powder yards themselves.

Around 1840, the artist Bass Otis painted a picture of the Elutherian Mills yards from a point on the opposite side of the creek, very near the spot where Charles Dalmas stood some thirty-six years earlier. In the Bass Otis view the powder yard retains much of the bucolic look of the earlier sketch, and does not look much like a major industry along the Brandywine. However, by this time

OVERLEAF: Charles Dalmas's sketch of the Du Pont Powder Yards in 1806. Copies of this were sent back to France to reassure worried stockholders.

INSET, OVERLEAF: Eleutherian Mills painted by Bass Otis around 1840.

the powder yards expanded south along the creek, and now included the Hagley Yard and the Lower Powder Yard, which was on the opposite side of the creek closer to Wilmington than Eleutherian Mills.[2]

All these pictures show an infant industry, but a substantial one by the standards of the time. Despite the ups and downs of the economy, the company was growing, due to the dogged determination of the owner-managers. By the beginning of the Civil War, the Du Pont Company had achieved a dominant position in the black powder industry in the United States. Despite this, not one photograph had been taken of the mills by 1860.

# The Birth of Photography

THE year 1839 saw the introduction of the first practical photographic process, the daguerreotype. People on both sides of the Atlantic Ocean soon were taking pictures photographically. "From today painting is dead!" declared French artist Paul Delaroche in a phrase more memorable than accurate. The first daguerreotypist to set up shop in Wilmington was C. P. Hogshead, who arrived in 1842 but stayed for only a short period. The daguerreotype process was clumsy and largely studio-bound, in that the silver plates on which the picture was taken had to be sensitized just before being exposed, a step that was much easier to do in a studio than out of doors. As a result, as Jack Hurley has pointed out, "relatively few photographs of industry have survived from the very earliest, pre-Civil War, period."[3] There are, as indicated above, no known views of the Du Pont Mills from that period.

Early photography captured the sense of American industry by capturing the faces of the people involved in it. The daguerreotype's greatest strength was in portraiture, and the Du Pont family was no different from others in rushing to have their pictures taken in studios in Wilmington, Philadelphia, and New York. Lammot, Alfred V., and E. I. du Pont, the three sons of Alfred Victor du Pont, head of the firm from 1837 to 1850, had their group portrait taken by William and Frederick Langenheim of Philadelphia around 1850. Samuel Francis and Sophie du Pont had their portraits made by J. Gurney of New York in 1853. Other du Pont family members patronized the studios of Elwood Garrett of Wilmington.

13

In the 1850s new forms of photography appeared, as inventors improved the process. One notable invention was the wet-plate negative, in which glass was coated with collodion (a solution of gun-cotton and ether) and then sensitized with silver nitrate. Wet-plate negatives made possible both ambrotypes (photographs made directly on glass) and paper prints, which could be made in large quantities from the same negative. The new paper photographs included cartes de visite (small portraits mounted on stiff card backings), large prints made on albumen paper, and stereo photographs. Of these, it was to be the stereo photograph that would have the first impact on industrial photography.

In the early 1850s stereo photography became very popular in Europe. Photographers discovered that they could stock and sell photographs of standard subjects, including travel photographs and views of public events such as fairs. Slowly this business spread to America. At first companies stocked European pictures, but gradually American photographers began supplying views of American scenery. By 1858 the stereo photograph was becoming a fad in America. Photographers traveled the country, searching for the picturesque. This work was interrupted by the Civil War, but in a way was also furthered by it. Along with the standard commercial work of taking portraits, firms like Matthew Brady's became famous for their stereo photographs of battlefields and war's aftermath. After the Civil War, this pent-up interest in seeing America was unleashed, and stereo photographs became ubiquitous. No scenic area was safe from the footsteps of the photographer carrying his wet-plate apparatus. Inevitably, sometime shortly after the Civil War, an unknown photographer traveled up the Brandywine Creek photographing a series of pictures that would be sold as a group titled "Beauties of the Brandywine." Thus was the first photograph of the Du Pont Company mills taken.

# The First Photographs
of the Du Pont Company

THE unknown photographer who took the pictures that comprise "The Beauties of the Brandywine" began his trip up the creek at the famous flour mills at Brandywine Village, where Market Street crossed the Brandywine. From there he proceeded upstream, photographing on both sides of the creek. His favorite artistic device was to place a person or group of people in the foreground, leaving the buildings in the background. Several of the pictures show only people and rocks and the Brandywine, the same people showing up over and over again in the pictures. Gradually he worked his way northward, photographing the Barley Mill in Wilmington and the raceway at Rockford near the Bancroft factory. Finally he reached the side of the creek opposite the Du Pont Lower Yard, near what is today the site of the Du Pont Company's Experimental Station. There he took eight stereo photographs showing the mill buildings, often artistically posing people in the foreground and giving the pictures dramatic captions.[4]

There is no indication on the stereos as to who published them, much less who took them, but the most likely photographer is Joseph Maybin. Little is known of Maybin except that he came to Wilmington sometime around 1865 and operated a studio there until 1888, specializing in "landscape" photography. James and Webb, a stationery store in Wilmington, published a series of stereo views by Maybin of "Wilmington and Vicinity" in 1873, and it is possible that the "Beauties of the Brandywine" was a precursor of that series.

For our purposes the most important photograph in the series is #262, "Rolling Mill, Du Pont's Powder Works," which gives a very clear view of a pair of rolling mills in the lower yard from across the creek. A lone man lounges on a flat rock in the foreground. The water in the creek is smoothed by a relatively long exposure time. On the opposite bank three workers stand patiently next to the mill. The large roll wheels show clearly within the mills. The three dimensional quality of the image when viewed stereoscopically is remarkable, and the detail in the picture is a gold mine of information for historians of the explosives industry. In addition, the photograph has much charm as a result of the rural setting (the hillside behind the mills is heavily wooded) and the calm figure in the foreground. This was the first of many photographs of the Du Pont mills and it is still one of the best. It was later published by the Union View Co. of

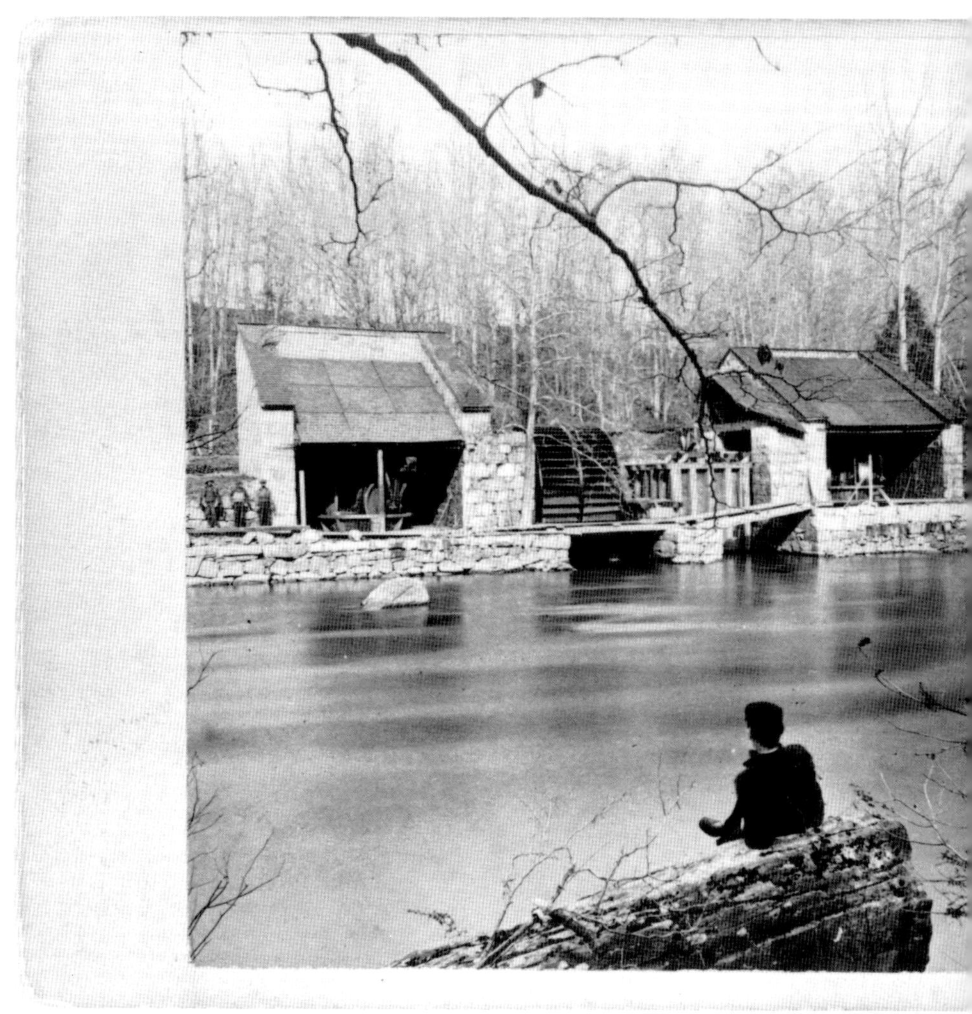

One of the series "Beauties of the Brandywine" by an unknown photographer, c. 1865. These stereo photographs were the first to show the powder mills.

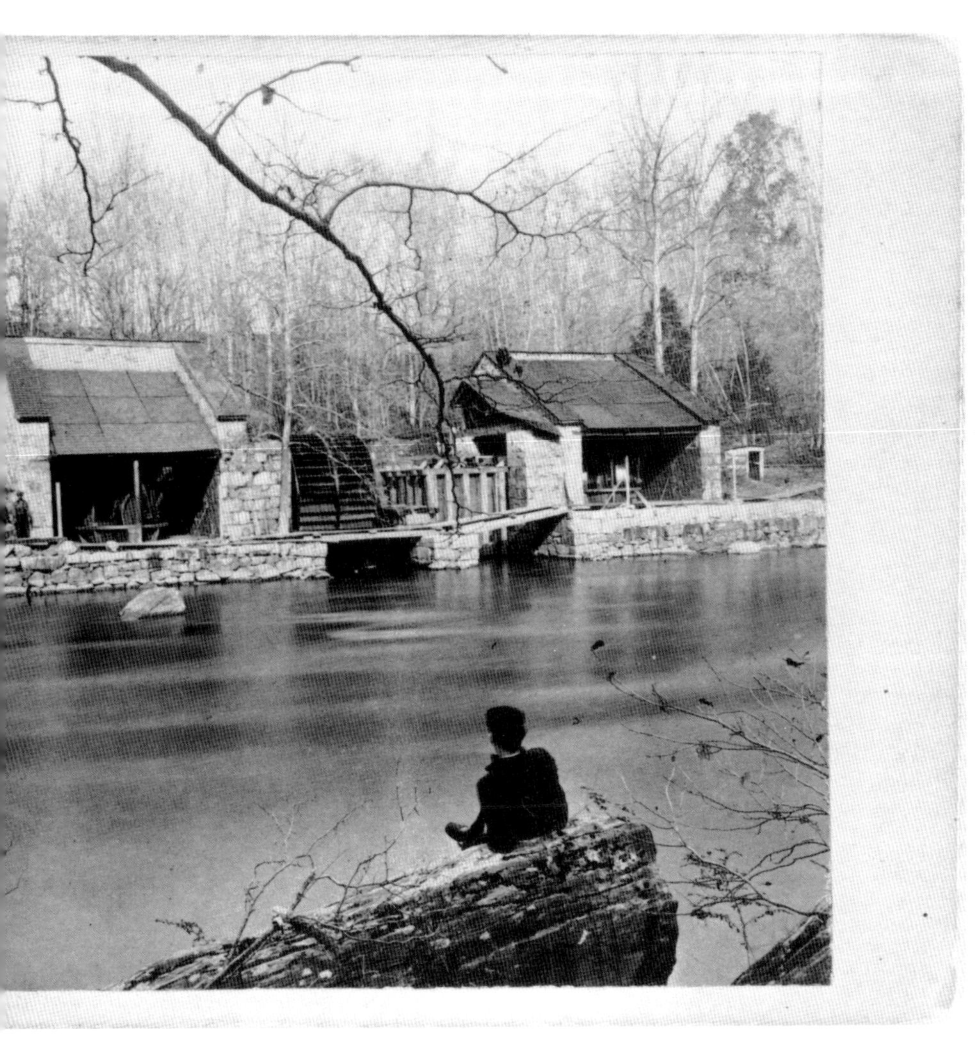

Rochester, N.Y. and titled "Brandywine Creek, Pennsylvania." Mislabeled or not, photography had come to the Du Pont Company.

After the Civil War, amateur photography in the United States developed on a limited basis. The wet-plate negative was still the chief form of photography, and this cumbersome and time-consuming process discouraged all but the most stout-hearted non-professionals from taking it up. In April of 1866 Wilmington photographer John Torbert wrote to Lammot du Pont that "as the season is opening when you may be experimenting in photography, if I can assist you please let me know." Nothing is known of the extent of Lammot du Pont's experiments in photography, but as he was the chief chemist for the company at that time, it was not unusual for him to be interested in the photographic process. Collodion, used in making wet-plate negatives, is very closely related to other nitro-cellulose products, such as dynamite, that were just then being developed. Lammot du Pont was certain to have the necessary chemicals already at hand for photography, and apparently he needed to acquire only cameras, trays, and glass in order to take pictures. Unfortunately, no photographs attributable to Lammot are known today, but his interest was passed on to his children. As we shall see, this played a vital role in the development of photography at Du Pont.

In 1877 Pierre Gentieu, a French immigrant who had been living in New York, came to Wilmington to go to work for the du Pont family in the powder yards. He had come to America around 1860, and he fought for the North in the Civil War. After he had worked a short while in the powder mills, the du Ponts recognized his merits and promoted him to an office job. For the rest of his life he remained a staunch du Pont loyalist, working in the powder yards until at least the first decade of the 1900s. He also took photographs.

Despite a sizeable correspondence with Francis G. du Pont which still survives, the origin of Gentieu's interest in photography is unknown, and there is little documentation of his methods and work. All we have are the outlines of his career and his photographs. We know that he began work at the yards in June 1877, but his earliest photography is dated 1883. He took pictures of the homes of Francis G. du Pont, Charles I. du Pont, Henry A. du Pont, and Eugene du Pont (all partners in the Du Pont Company), as well as pictures of their families. In addition, he took pictures of the families of Du Pont mill workers who lived in the village of Henry Clay, along the banks of the Brandywine close

Scene in the woods near the Brandywine Creek, attributed to Henry B. du Pont, c. 1895. The gentleman near the camera is unidentified, but could possibly be Pierre Gentieu.

18

to the works. These family pictures are rich social documents of life in a mill village of the 1880s through the early years of this century.

More important for the history of the Du Pont Company are the photographs that Gentieu took of workers, machinery, and buildings in the powder yards themselves. The purpose of these photographs is obscure. That Gentieu was an artist of some skill is obvious from a sketch that he drew of the Lower Yard in 1878. Photography was evidently for him an extension of this artistic creativity. That the du Pont family members who ran the company knew of and encouraged Gentieu's photography is also obvious from the patronage that they gave him to take pictures of their homes and families. Gentieu took many group portraits of employees in the powder yards that would have involved a considerable amount of time away from the job to pose and expose. This interruption of worktime was condoned by the owners, but no official use of any of these pictures is evident. There were as yet no company publications or outlets for printing these pictures, but they were in a way an employee relations effort on the part

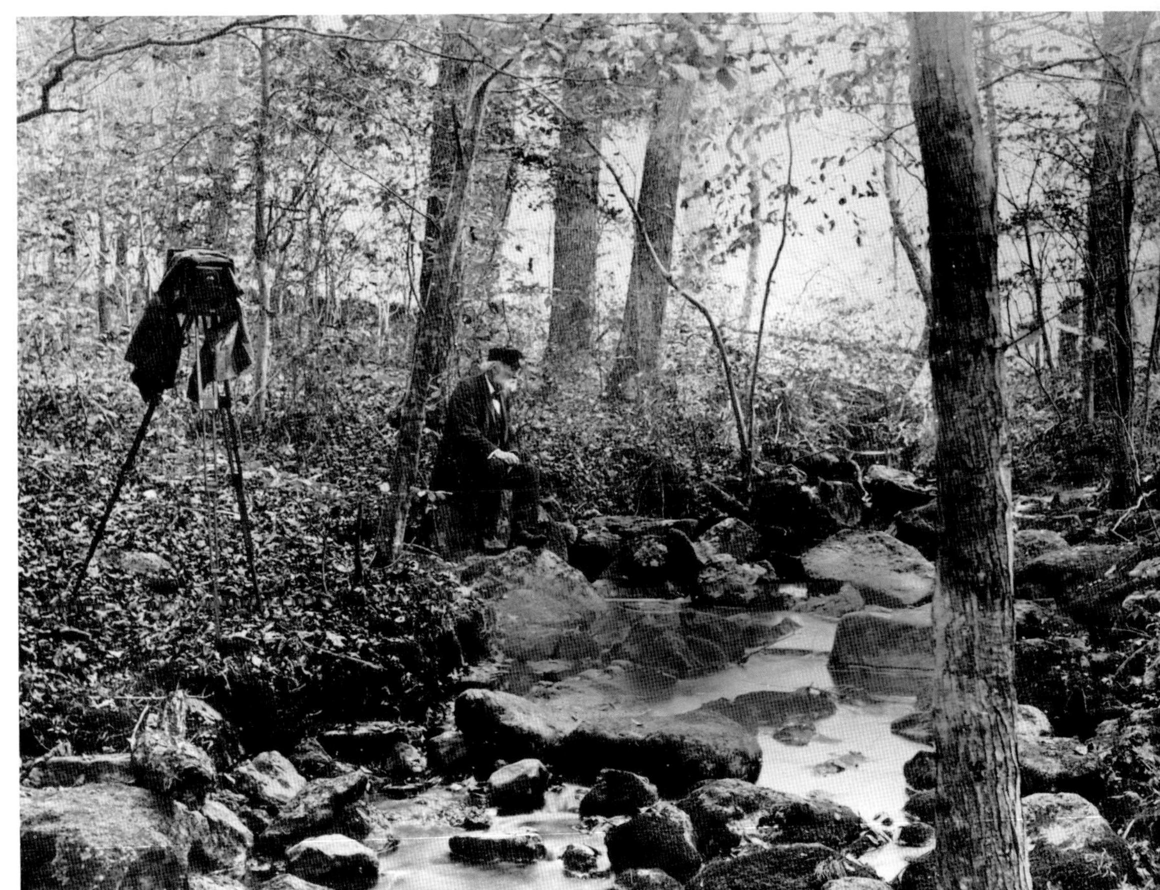

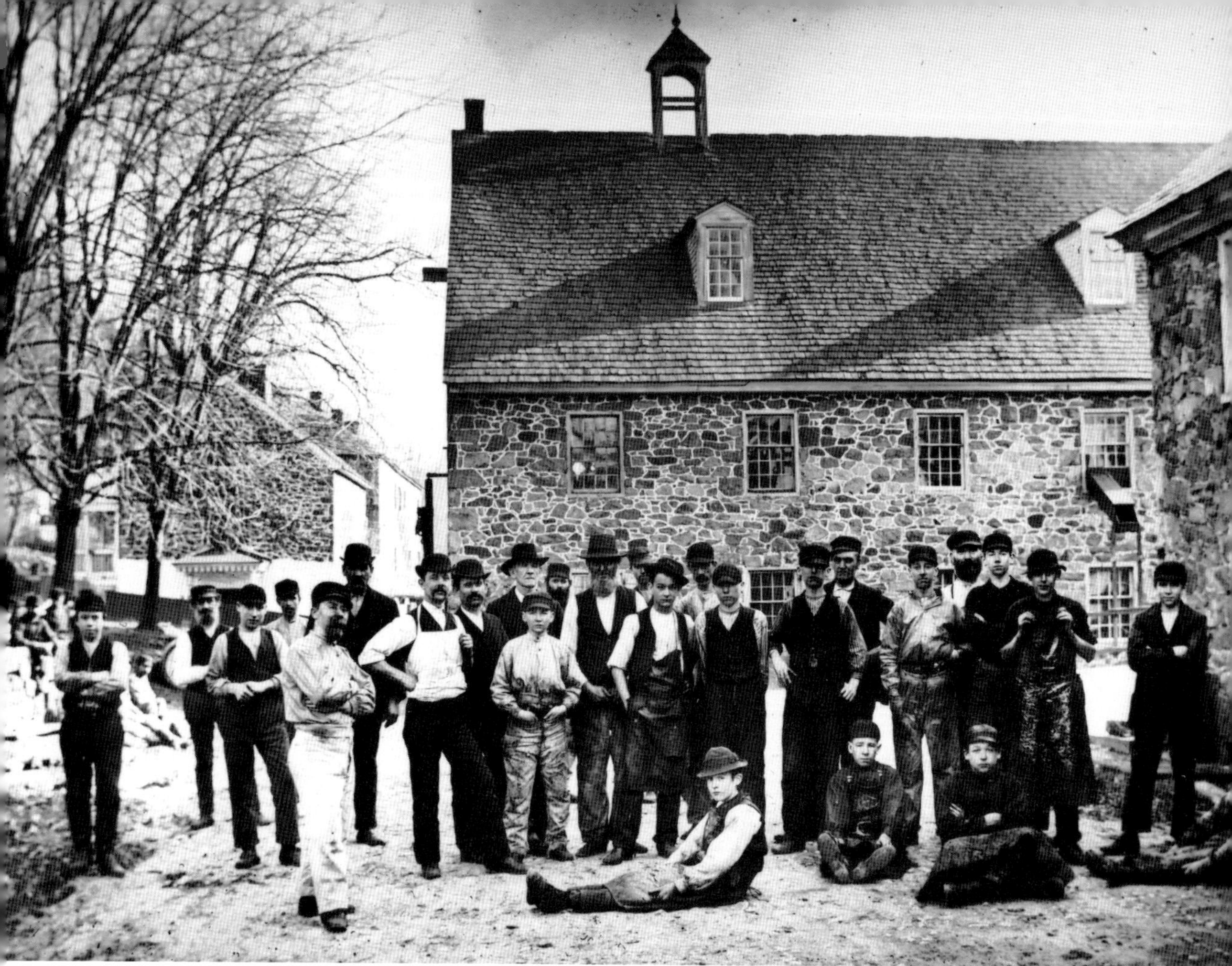

Workers at a keg mill near the Du Pont powder yards photographed by Pierre Gentieu, c. 1900.

of the company. A group portrait promotes a feeling of togetherness in any assemblage, and Gentieu's pictures show a deep sense of comraderie. Copies of these prints found their way into albums belonging to du Pont family members, but it is not known if copies were sold or given to the workers themselves. Presumably Gentieu sold some of his prints, such as one of the Tippecanoe Harrison and Morton Club of Du Pont's Banks, taken in September of 1888 in Henry Clay Village. There is an indication that Francis G. du Pont frequently paid Gentieu for photographs, but no record of prices survives.

Pierre Gentieu's photographic record of the Du Pont powder mills is rich and extremely valuable. Pierre S. du Pont purchased around 350 Gentieu negatives from Gentieu's children in 1946, and gave them to the library of the Historical Society of Delaware. A set of original prints made from them is in the Hagley Museum and Library, and provides an invaluable resource on the history of the yards. Much of the restoration work done at Hagley would have been impossible were it not for Gentieu's work.

There are more than 150 prints of views by Pierre Gentieu of the Du Pont yards and the nearby area along the Brandywine Creek. These date from 1883 to 1917, and they show a wide variety of subjects. Rolling mills, powder wagons, employee groups, narrow gauge railroad cars, and offices are some of the items covered. In addition to the lives of the workers in the mills, the lives of families at home are also documented. Gentieu's photography was very straight forward, with simple camera angles and poses dictated not only by his equipment, but also by his clearminded approach. He was a gifted amateur photographer who desired to show things distinctly in his pictures. For this he was encouraged by the officers of the Du Pont Company, and we can be thankful that he has left us the benefit of his vision. His photography was to leave its mark in the history of the company he worked for so faithfully for so long.

# A Hobby or a Tool?

AFTER the Civil War, the Du Pont Company, despite fits and starts in the economy, continued its growth, and remained a very centralized and family-run firm. Henry du Pont, the head of the company, resisted in many ways new developments in the explosives industry. At the same time, however, he was determined to rationalize and even dominate that industry. Change happened in spite of him. The younger generation, represented by Lammot du Pont and Francis G. du Pont, looked forward eagerly to improvements in blasting powders and high explosives, and in 1880 Lammot started the Repauno Chemical Company, makers of dynamite. Though not an official part of the Du Pont Company, this was backed by the big three explosives firms in the country at the time, Du Pont, the Hazard Powder Company, and the Laflin & Rand Company. In 1888 Francis G. du Pont went to Mooar, Iowa, to build the then largest blasting powder plant in the world. Coming back east in 1890, he developed the plant at Carney's Point, New Jersey, to make smokeless powder.

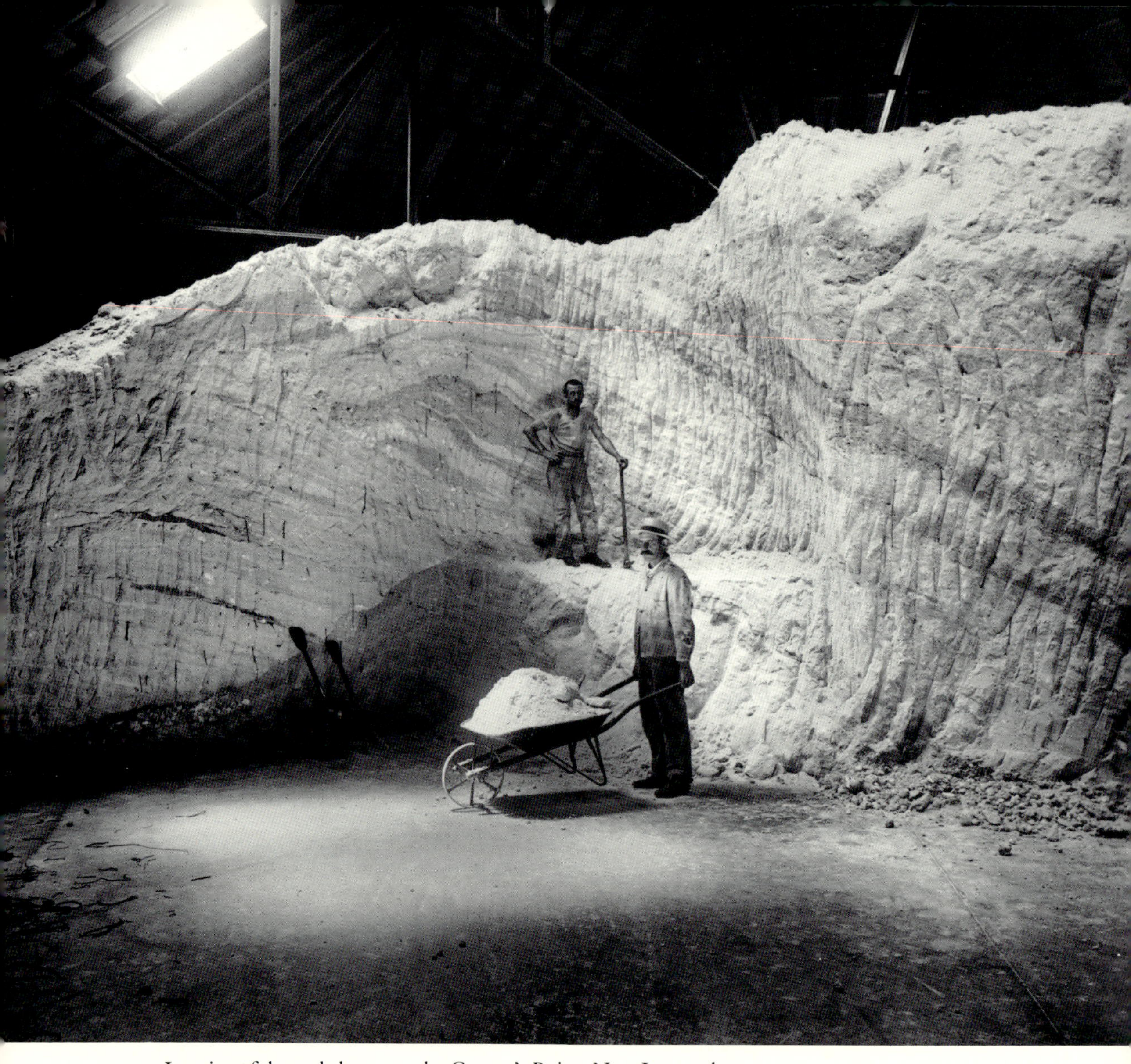

Interior of the soda house at the Carney's Point, New Jersey plant,
possibly taken by Francis G. du Pont, c. 1895.

There exist glass plate negatives dating from the early 1890s of the Carney's Point plant, by an unknown photographer. They may well have been the work of Francis G. du Pont himself. He was an avid astronomer and is known to have taken his own telescopic photographs. His work with Pierre Gentieu indicates a general interest in company photography as well. There are no photographs of Repauno or the Mooar plants from the time of their construction, so that the Carney's Point photographs are the earliest known use by the Du Pont Company of pictures to document a distant plant for the home office. They were taken, however, simply for Francis G.'s own interest and not as part of any official effort by the company. Harry Haskell, Sr. later wrote that at this time, "the business was conducted by a few people who around-the-table read all the mail and attended to everything in somewhat haphazard fashion."[5] The company's use of photography was no different.

Throughout this period competition in the powder industry was regulated through the Gunpowder Trade Association, dominated by the three companies listed above. This Association functioned relatively efficiently to control prices and divide markets, obviating the need for any type of active advertising, a "science" soon to burst upon the American scene. Techniques for mechanical reproduction of photographs remained primitive, and their use in industry before the twentieth century was very limited. Other explosives firms such as Hazard and the Aetna Powder Company of Indiana, did, however, compile albums of large photographic prints to show off their facilities. There is no indication that the Du Pont Company did likewise until well into the twentieth century. By then both Hazard and Aetna had been acquired by Du Pont, which had come to totally dominate the industry after 1902. Along with these companies and others like them came traditions of company use of photographs new to Du Pont. These trends of expansion and acquisition brought new ideas to the Du Pont Company on the use of photography. Another source of ideas was to come from within the Du Pont family. The new generation was to have definite ideas on business that would shape the company in the new century.

In November 1888 Henry Belin du Pont, son of Lammot du Pont (who had died in an explosion in 1884), wrote to his older brother Pierre from school in Andover, Massachusetts. "I only can think of a few things [for Christmas]" he reported, "a detective camera [and] two things to hold photographs." The year 1888 was a watershed in photography, for it was then that George Eastman introduced his first Kodak camera, which used film negatives. A detective camera was a name for any small, usually hand-held, camera that could unobtrusively take pictures. These had come into existence around 1881, using the new dry-

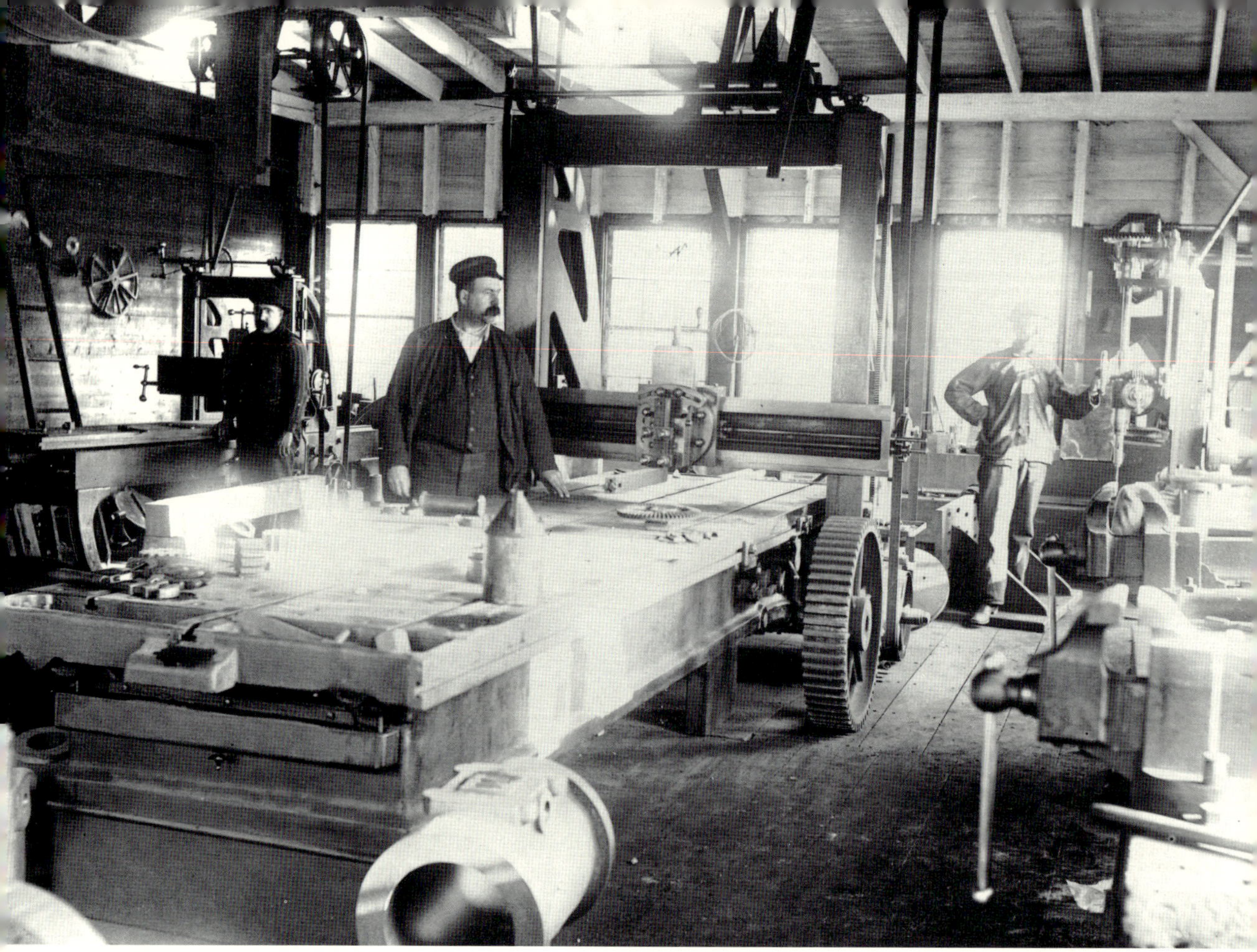

ABOVE: Machine shop at the Hazard Powder Company plant in Hazardville, Connecticut, from an album of views of the plant by an unknown photographer, c. 1900.

RIGHT: A.G. Faye at work in the office of the Aetna Dynamite Works, Aetna, Indiana, March 1895. Photograph by Edward Harrington, plant manager.



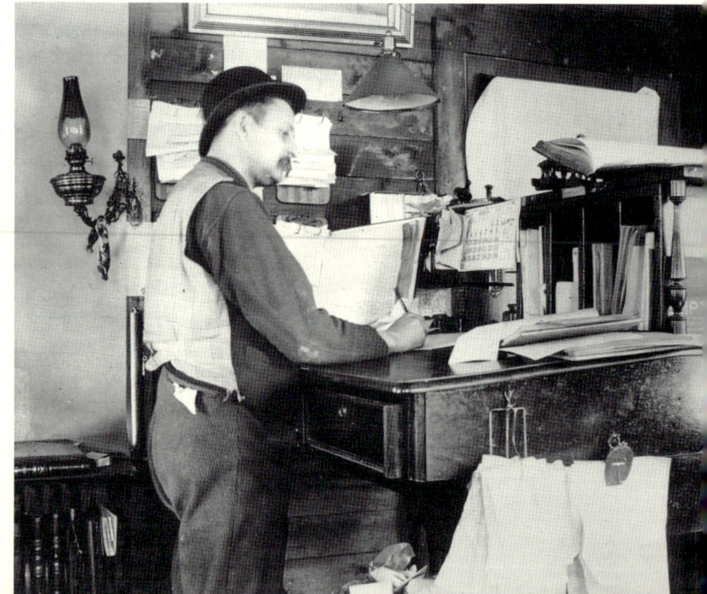

plate glass negatives that had replaced wet-plate ones. Dry plates could be stored for long periods of time before use, and they did not have to be prepared by the photographer right before the picture was taken. Eastman took this a step further, and provided a camera that was simplicity itself to use. The entire camera was sent back to the Eastman Company to have the film developed and a new roll inserted. The amateur could know practically nothing and still take a picture. Many Americans saw this as a great improvement.

Many members of the du Pont family who were interested in chemistry became interested in the new fad of photography. Chief among these were the children of Lammot du Pont, principally Pierre S., Henry B., and Irénée. The photographs in the Hagley Museum and Library attributed to Pierre S. du Pont consist mainly of travel snapshots, many of the 1893 World's Fair in Chicago. Pierre worked at Carney's Point and then at the powder yards in Delaware for nine years before leaving the company and heading to Louisville to seek his fortune. He would be back.

Henry B. du Pont, on the other hand, developed tuberculosis and died at an early age. However, he spent his time after graduating from school on the banks of the Brandywine, and while there took some of the loveliest pictures that exist of the Brandywine valley in the nineteenth century. He lived in Louviers, across the creek from the powder yards, and often walked about them taking pictures, sometimes accompanied by his wife, Eleuthera Bradford du Pont. Usually the powder yards served as a background for a portrait of his wife or his friends, but the quality of the pictures and the care of their composition bespeaks more than a causal involvement in their taking. Henry Belin du Pont and Pierre Gentieu rank as the two major photographers of the Du Pont Company in the nineteenth century. Belin du Pont had to leave Delaware for his health, and died in Arizona in 1902. But a new century was about to dawn.

Another death in that year was that of Eugene du Pont, the president of the company. This left the company without a clear successor to head the business. The dramatic story of how Alfred I. du Pont, a younger partner in the firm, stepped in with an offer to buy the company, has been often told.[7] The crisis was weathered, and the hundred-year old company remained in the hands of the younger generation of the family, led by cousins Pierre, Alfred I., and T. Coleman du Pont. This new generation had new ideas on how a business should be run. Coleman and Pierre received their business education chiefly in the rough and tumble growth industries of street railways and steel in the Midwest. New techniques in office management, in fiscal administration, and in organization and marketing were some of the fresh ideas brought in by the cousins. New approaches

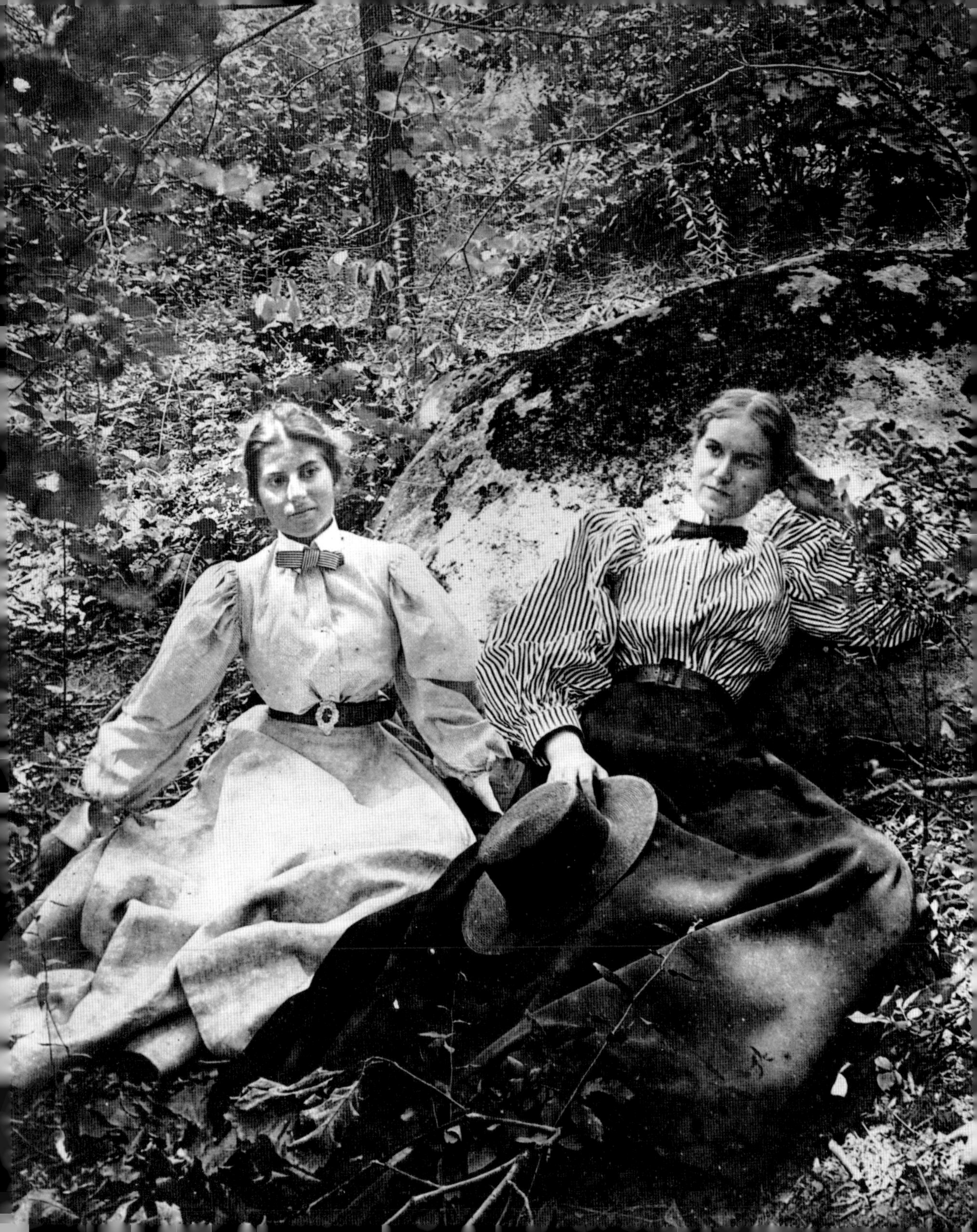

in photography were to play an increasingly important part in the actual, day-to-day running of the company. The photographs of Du Pont from the nineteenth century are rare but valuable artifacts which help tell the story of the company, but had little to do with its actual functioning. In the twentieth century, photographs from the Du Pont Company were to become increasingly abundant and show not only what the company was doing, but actually play a purposeful function in that operation. The twentieth century is the true age of industrial photography.

The new century brought an increased picture consciousness not only to industry but to the American people as a whole. Photographs were becoming commonplace. "The advent of the simple snapshot camera and its associated roll film" write Brian Coe and Paul Gates, "brought about important changes in attitudes toward photography, and these changes came swiftly."[8] Everyone could now be his own photographer, and people came to expect photographs to be used as illustrations. Although the heydey of photojournalism was to come in the 1920s and 30s, the first daily newspaper illustrated entirely with photographs, the *London Daily Mirror,* began in 1904. In addition, the 1890s saw the beginnings of motion pictures which by 1910 were the major form of mass entertainment in this country. It was in this period that "in the hands of skilled photographers, the camera was starting to do more than just record. It was starting to lead."[9]

The new leadership of the Du Pont Company was well aware of these developments in American society at the turn of the century, and among the new ideas that they brought to the company was an increase in the appreciation and utilization of photography as a medium of communication. At first, photos were used for internal company information, but as the new technology for printing photographs developed, they were used increasingly for getting the Du Pont Company message to the public.

"We have not the slightest idea what we are buying," said Pierre du Pont in 1902 when he, Alfred I. and T. Coleman du Pont purchased the Du Pont Company, and they were not the only ones in the dark. "I think the old company also has a very slim idea of the property they possess," he added.[10] The new owners' aim was to bring what was then a "cartel of small family firms" into the twentieth century of business practices. To do this, they "brought the ways of both Carnegie and [Frederick Winslow] Taylor to the Du Pont Company, mod-

Eleuthera B. du Pont (Mrs. H.B. du Pont) [left] and an unidentified companion in the woods near Louviers along the Brandywine. Photograph by H.B. du Pont, c. 1895.

ifying them to meet the special needs of the explosives industry."[11] But before they could accomplish that, they had to find out exactly what they had bought. To do that they turned, in part, to photography.

In 1899 Pierre had been instrumental in setting up the Manufacturers Contracting Company, an "independent" design and construction firm. The president of the company was William H. Fenn, Jr., who had been Pierre's roommate at M.I.T.; treasurer was Irénée du Pont, Pierre's brother. They did some work for Pierre in Louisville, and when the cousins bought the Du Pont Company in 1902, one of the first jobs that the Manufacturers Contracting Company got was to remodel Coleman's house on Broom Street in Wilmington. This handy firm was a precursor of the Du Pont Company Engineering Department. As such, they received a very important commission from Du Pont in 1903: to survey all the black powder plants owned or controlled by the company.

There were a lot of them, for in 1903 the cousins completed their first important step in the consolidation of the explosives industry in America. As Du Pont already had a controlling share of the Hazard Powder Company, the cousins realized early on that control of the Laflin & Rand Company, the third big explosives manufacture in the U.S. at the beginning of the twentieth century, was the key to the industry. By purchasing Laflin & Rand, Du Pont obtained a majority interest in practically every black powder maker in the country, as well as in many high explosives businesses. Unraveling the legal tangle of who owned what shares in what company was the task of Pierre and Coleman. To operate all these interests, they set up the E. I. du Pont de Nemours Powder Company. In an account of expenses for that company there is an item on September 24, 1903 for $340.09 for the Manufacturers Contracting Company appraisal of the black powder plants and one later in March of 1904 for $2,624.78 for appraisal of the other plants. This appraisal included the first systematic photographic survey of all the Du Pont properties.

The two albums of pictures from this survey each contain about 200 photographs, each print being 3¼" × 4¼". Duplicate albums were produced and distributed to company executives. Pictures show plants at such faraway places as Punxatawney, Pennsylvania, and Keokuk, Iowa. In many of the pictures the same two gentlemen, presumably employees of the Manufacturers Contracting Company, show up with notebooks and pencils in hand, jotting down notes and measurements for the appraisal.

The pictures' size (3¼" × 4¼") is an indication that they were taken with Kodak #3 cameras, either the pocket folding or the cartridge varieties. These were very convenient, easy-to-use cameras that were to play a big role in engineering site photography for the Du Pont Company. They took film negatives (the cartridge would also take glass plate negatives, but the casualness of the pictures in the survey leads one to believe that roll film probably was used), and these original negatives have disappeared. The photographs are mounted in ready-made albums specifically designed for that size print, and are numbered on the negative. A detailed, typed list of the prints is tipped in the back of every album. In one album, this list is typed on Irénée du Pont's letterhead, indicating that he was perhaps in some way responsible for the production of the albums. Soon it was to become standard practice to record distant plants for the home office using photographs, but these 1903 albums represent a new step at Du Pont: for the first time, the modern method of photography was being used in an official company capacity.

Other uses for photography were being found within the new firm. The Sales Department of E. I. du Pont de Nemours Powder Company was a conglomerate of the sales departments of all the companies that had been consolidated. It was large, unwieldy, and full of duplications of effort. The task of straightening out this mess was assigned to Amory Haskell, who became Vice-President for sales. He instituted annual sales department conventions, the first of which met in New York in 1904. Salesmen and company experts gave practical lectures on products, especially blasting powder and high explosives. After one lecturer at the 1905 convention in Indianapolis had illustrated his talk by holding up small photographic prints, Haskell rose and urged the adoption of newer methods. "I would like to say that we should be glad when any paper is being prepared if the writer would forward to us photographs or illustrations ahead of time so that lantern slides could be made of them," he declared. "I think illustrations shown at the time reference is made to them add very much to the interest of the papers and elucidate them greatly; so I hope you gentlemen in the future will feel free to send to headquarters of the Sales Department such illustrations as you may wish to have made into lantern slides."

Salesmen were quick to get the message, and the published proceedings of the next year's convention in Washington, D.C. were printed on glossy paper and amply illustrated, the most extensive use of pictures being in a lecture by Francis I. du Pont on the new laboratories at the Experimental Station in Wilmington. (These are the earliest known pictures of that facility.) Also in 1905 Dr. Charles L. Reese, head of the Eastern Laboratory at Repauno, read a paper on "So-called Safety or Flameless Explosives." This talk was illustrated with photographs of tests of gunpowders at night, showing the flashes of the explosions. Aside from some of Francis G. du Pont's photographs of testing equipment, these

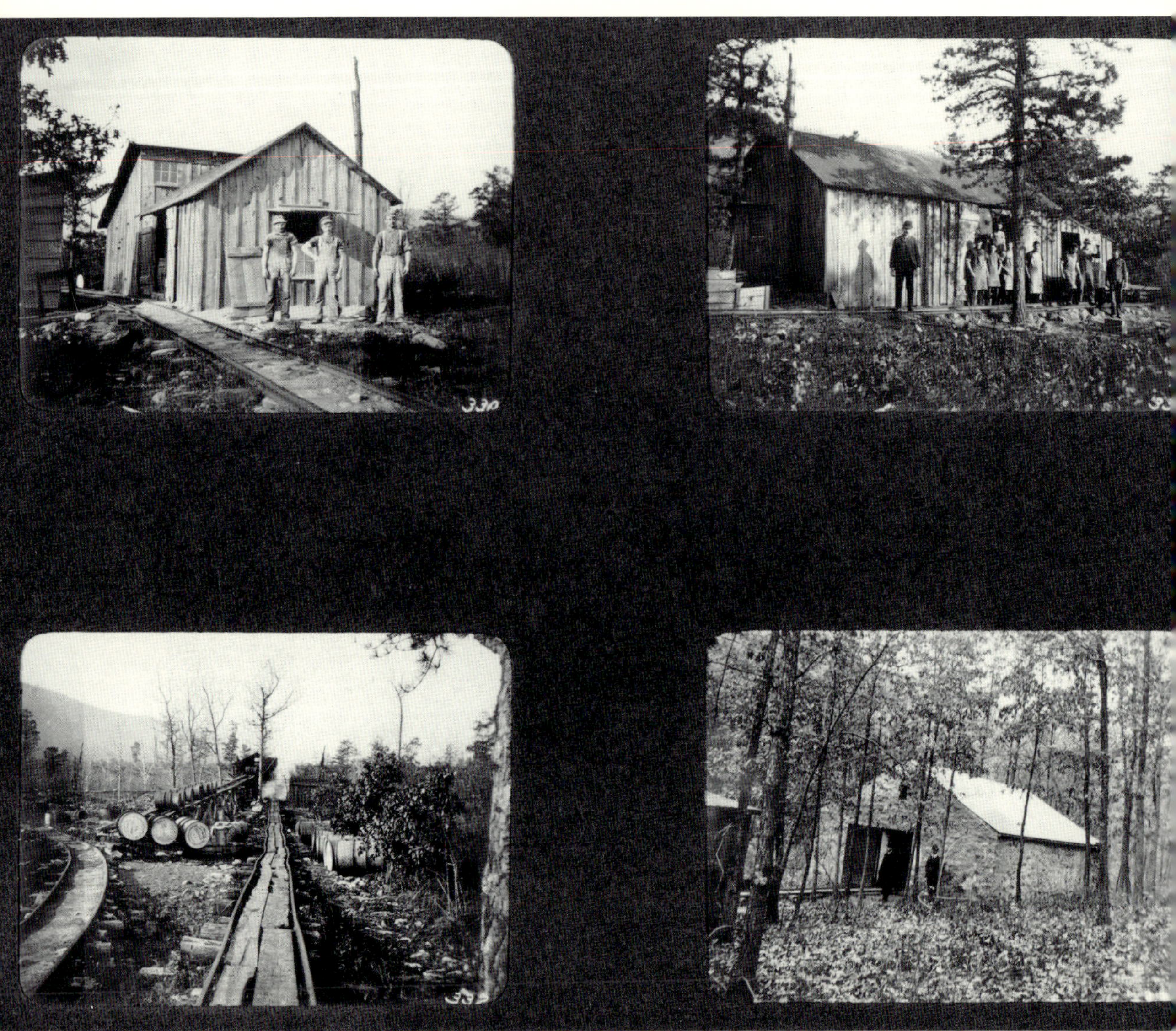

A page from the photograph album from the 1903 survey of Du Pont Company holdings. This was the first systematic use of photographs in appraising company properties. Shown on this page are views of the Enterprise Powder Company in Luzerne County, Pennsylvania.

Page from photograph album, DETAIL.

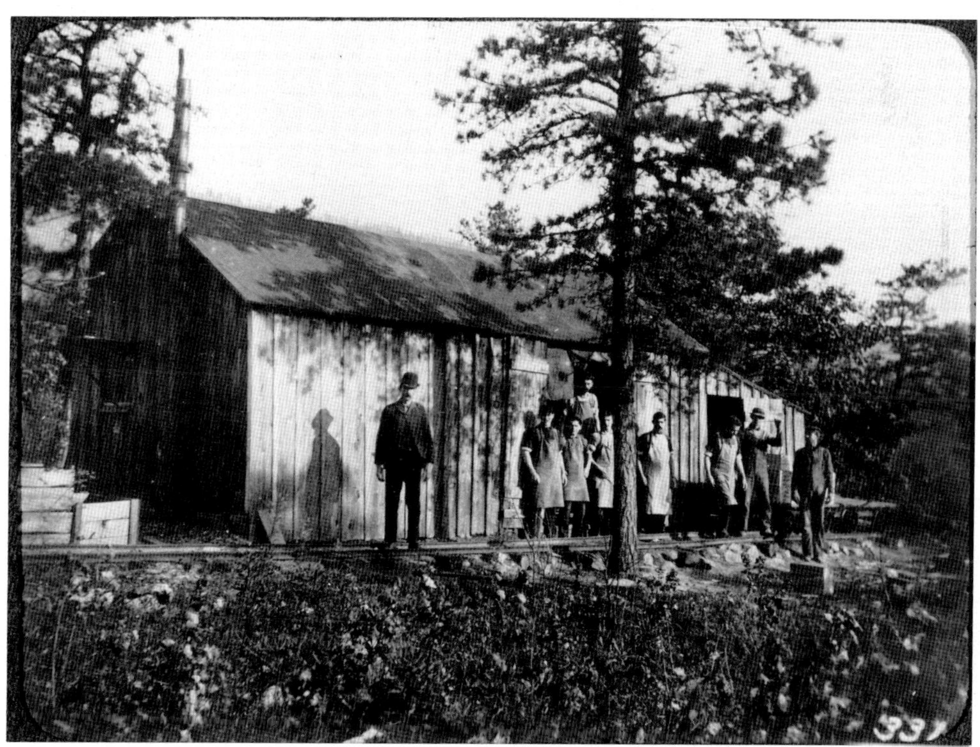

are the earliest examples of the scientific use of photographs within the company research branch.

In 1905 Pierre S. du Pont traveled to Europe and South America, principally on business, but with plenty of time reserved for sightseeing. He took along his camera. An album of photographs from Argentina and Chile exists from this trip, and one picture shows Pierre walking along a street in Buenos Aires with a Kodak Folding Pocket Camera under his arm. The size of the other pictures in the album indicates that this would have been the Kodak #3 again, the same model used to survey the company's holdings in 1903. Several of the snapshots in the album show that Pierre had a flair for taking pictures, and there are many views of plantings and vegetation, which perhaps he referred to in his later development of the gardens and conservatory at Longwood.

The most important outcome of this trip for the Du Pont Company, however, was a report which Pierre sent to the Executive Committee on his return concerning the nitrate fields of Chile. This was a 45-page report illustrated with his own photographs taken in the nitrate fields, many of which also appear in the album he kept for himself. Although the company took no action on purchasing any of this land in 1905, a few years later (in 1910) Du Pont did make a move in Chile, purchasing what was to become the Oficina Delaware nitrate field. This continuing interest in South America produced a flood of photographs in various reports back to the home office, and once the field was purchased, photographs were heavily used to show the executives in Wilmington progress in construction and production.

By this time the use of photographs was being systematized within the company. Although each operating department of the company (Black Powder, High Explosives, and Smokeless Powder) maintained its own engineering division until 1911, a standard form was developed in 1909 for sending photographs of construction progress back to the home office. This was the ubiquitous Form 6277Y envelope,  made from brown stock and measuring $5\frac{1}{4} \times 8$ inches, with spaces on the front for writing the name of the works and the structure represented in the photograph (or photographs) enclosed in the form. There were also spaces for the date of the photograph and the monthly report with which the picture was included, the name of the photographer, and a space for "remarks." Each of these envelopes was numbered by the home office when received.

The idea was that engineers on site would take their own pictures and have them developed, sending prints in with their reports. The company apparently

A team of surveyors at Eastern Laboratory, Repauno, New Jersey, c. 1900.

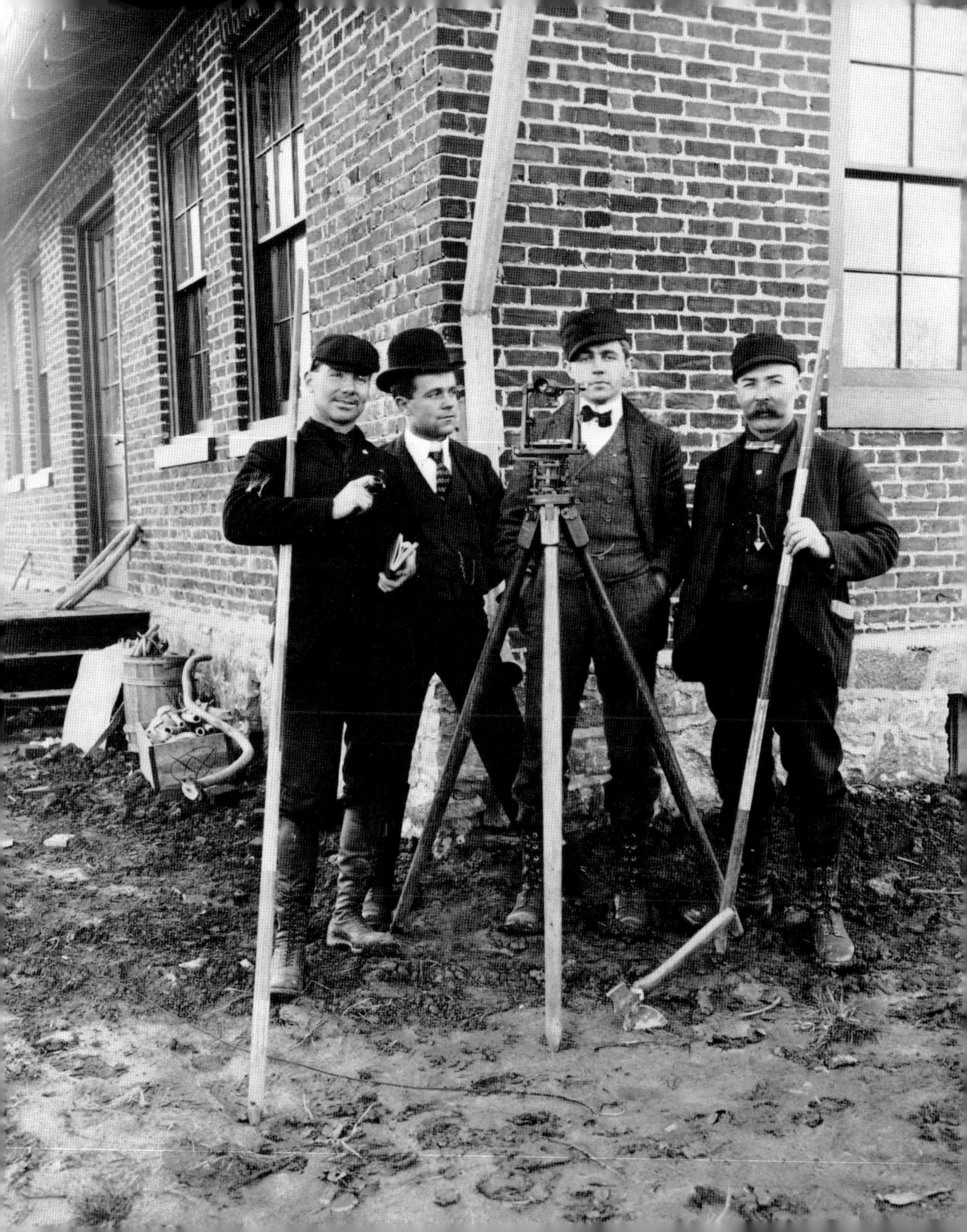

expected that the photographs would be small enough to fit within the envelopes, but some engineers insisted on using larger format cameras, and some even hired local professional photographers to do the job. Some of these prints were too large for the standard envelopes. When a general engineering department for the entire company was finally set up in 1911, they responded to this bureaucratic problem by issuing a set of regulations on Standard Practices, including a section on photography. "It will be the duty of all men in charge of Construction work," the company declared, "to take photographs periodically on all projects where any material progress has been made. The general custom is to take photographs on the dates Semi-monthly Physical Progress Reports are due, i.e., the 25th of each month . . . Before deviating from the usual practice, instructions will be secured from the Wilmington Office." To insure similar sizes for all photography received, the department decreed that "The #3-A Eastman Autographic Kodak is the standard size, and Resident Engineers not suitably equipped with such Kodaks will communicate with Wilmington Office, and arrangements will be made to have them furnished with same." The Kodak was now the official camera of the Du Pont Company!

The Kodak Folding Pocket #3–A camera was introduced by the Eastman Kodak Company in 1903. It produced a slightly larger picture size than the earlier #3, i.e. $3\frac{1}{4}'' \times 5\frac{1}{2}''$, the same size as a standard postcard of the day. It took #122 film, from which one could get ten exposures on a roll. The basic model went through many changes, including different lens and shutter combinations, but it always remained popular because of the large picture size and the ease of use. In 1914 Kodak introduced the autographic feature, by means of which identification could be written on the negative at the time of exposure by opening a small cover on the back. This made it even more useful for technical photography in the hands of amateurs (such as Du Pont Company engineers), and in 1916 the Model #3–A became the first camera ever equipped with a coupled range finder for accurate focusing. This sturdy camera remained a popular workhorse for the Du Pont Company well into the 1930s.

The Engineering Department's Standard Practices also mentioned that "panoramic photographs should be forwarded to Wilmington Office in one package, rolled face out." This was the first appearance of a form of photography—panoramic views—that was to become heavily used by Du Pont.

The photographs sent in by field engineers to the home office are documentary photography in its most basic form. Most would not be classified as good pictures, but they are full of details of construction and industrial scenes that provide historians with much information on technology. Occasionally a picture contains (usually inadvertently) staff at work, but most show construction projects in progress devoid of human presence. The Du Pont Company Engineering Department collection at the Hagley Museum and Library contains approximately 15,000 of these photographs, still resting securely in their form 6277Y envelopes.

While the Engineering Department was setting guidelines for its photography, other sections of the company were increasing their use of photography drastically. In 1907 the Sales Department began a promotional effort to encourage trap shooting, as it was felt that the demand for gunpowder for hunting had peaked. This, according to the company itself (in an article on Du Pont advertising published in 1919), was the "first organized effort by the Du Pont Company to use advertising in a constructive and promotional way," and marked the advent of photography in Du Pont advertising. Pictures of champion trap shooters began appearing in advertisements, along with photographs of the competitions themselves. The assumed success of this program led to a broad evaluation of Du Pont advertising practices and to the eventual appointment in 1911 of George Frank Lord as the first Advertising Manager. The next big campaign was a promotion of dynamite as a farm tool for clearing land and digging ditches. This campaign also used photographs of stump blasting and similar activities.

By 1920 the Advertising Department of the Du Pont Company had a staff of about 200, and was distributing one and one-quarter million pieces of direct advertising a month. They maintained a "photograph gallery" in their office headquarters, which was in a building half a mile from the Du Pont headquarters in Wilmington. This was a picture library, which maintained files of photographs procured mostly from photographers outside of the company.

Another step in the company's use of photographs came in July 1913 when Du Pont began publication of the *Du Pont Magazine*. By 1919 the firm claimed that "we publish the most pretentious house organ produced." Presumably by "pretentious" they meant elaborate and prestigious, although at times it is hard to be sure. The first issue of the *Du Pont Magazine* was 5½″ × 8½″ and contained 32 pages, with thirteen very small black and white photographs reproduced. Eight of these photographs were of trap shooting and two were of ditch digging with dynamite, following the two major promotional campaigns at the time. The magazine maintained this size and general content through 1916, when it suspended publication for one year. Publication was renewed in 1918, and the magazine was then larger (9″ × 12″), had full color reproductions of paintings on its covers, and used more and larger photographs. The first issue in the new format contained 32 photographs, with only three of trap shooting.

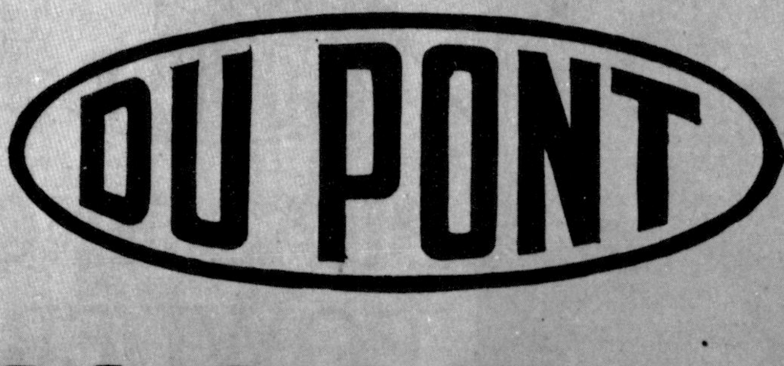



# MAGAZINE

**AND AGRICULTURAL BLASTER**

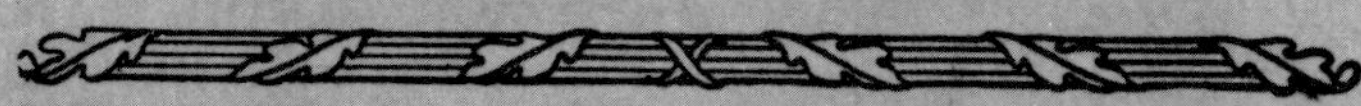

| Vol. 1 | JULY, 1913 | No. 1 |

## The Du Pont Army

## Carrying the Powder to Perry

## Exiling the Thawing Kettle

## Explosives as Life Insurers

## Farming With Dynamite

## The Portable Gun Club

## Manufactured Leather in the Automobile Industry

**PUBLISHED MONTHLY**

COPYRIGHTED, 1913

## E. I. du Pont de Nemours Powder Company

ESTABLISHED 1802                    WILMINGTON, DEL.

# DU PONT MAGAZINE

Vol. 7     AUGUST, 1916     No. 8

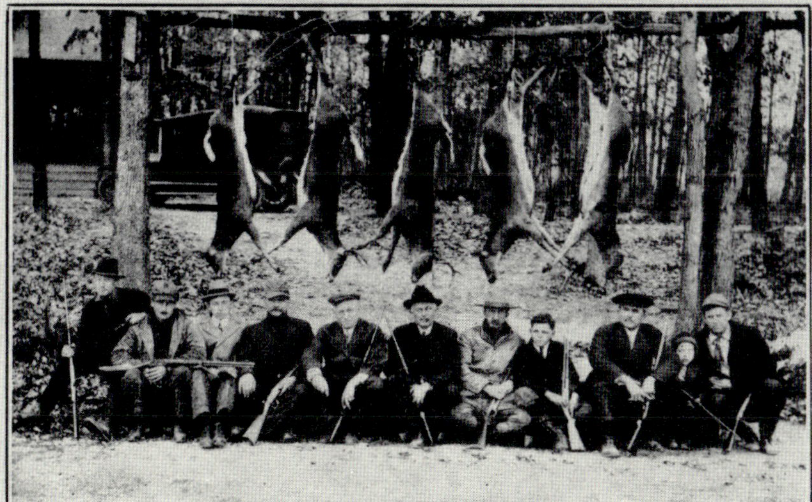

A PENNSYLVANIA DEER HUNT

## PUBLISHED MONTHLY



### E. I. du Pont de Nemours & Company

ESTABLISHED 1802       WILMINGTON, DEL.

In an attempt to collect appropriate advertising photographs, the Advertising Division sponsored a photograph contest starting in May 1918. Pictures were to show a variety of subjects including agricultural and industrial uses of explosives, painting, or leather substitutes. Employees of the company were ineligible, and the pictures were to be judged on their merit as advertising pictures, and not as art. All entries became the property of the Du Pont Company, which reserved all publishing rights. In January 1919 the winners were announced, H.M. Magie of Waynesboro, Virginia taking first prize of $100 for a picture showing the use of agricultural explosives. Unfortunately, if this picture or any of the other 694 photographs entered was ever used by Du Pont in advertising, it was not identified as being so from the contest, so it is now impossible to identify the prize winning pictures. Judging from other pictures of agricultural uses of explosives appearing in the *Du Pont Magazine,* chances are that the contest entries were not terribly exciting or attractive. The judges were looking for "good contrast," and the pictures were to be "clear and sharp and *in focus.*" These were evidently the marks of a good advertising photograph in 1918.

Along with the Advertising Department, which was started in 1911, a Publicity Bureau was established by the company in 1916. This was partially the result of some unfavorable publicity the company was receiving during the early years of World War I, and partially in response to a felt need to take better advantage of public relations media to support Du Pont. Eventually, in the 1920s and 30s, the Publicity Bureau (which became the Publicity Department in 1935) was to become a major user of photographs within the company, but first the Du Pont Company underwent the turmoil of world war. This world-wide catastrophe meant a tremendous growth in demand for military powders, and the Du Pont Company began an unprecedented construction program to meet first the needs of the Allies, and in 1917, the needs of the United States for more explosives. To keep track of this growth, increasing use of photography was necessary, and as a step in that direction, the company made use of a man already on their payroll.

OVERLEAF, LEFT: The cover of the first *Du Pont Magazine,* July 1913. This issue was illustrated inside with small reproductions of photographs of trap shooting and land clearing.

OVERLEAF, RIGHT: The first *Du Pont Magazine* to have a photograph on its cover, August 1916.

# Du Pont's First Professional Photographer

WHEN the Du Pont Company hired its first full-time photographer in 1915, it acquired an energetic and seasoned professional in thirty-five year old John A. Dick. Mr. Dick's experience included industrial and commercial photography, operation of his own studio, and travel as a demonstrating salesman for two major photographic firms, Kodak and Ansco. This experience was immediately put to use, and for the next twenty-eight years he made a major contribution in taking photography within the Du Pont Company from an avocation to an important research and communications tool in the hands of professionals.

John Dick's first assignment was to take "mug" shots for photo identification badges issued to the thousands of workers in the vast, smokeless power plant being built at Carney's Point, New Jersey to supply World War I needs. Not only did all employees have to wear such identification, but the act of photographing job seekers was considered one way of screening potential saboteurs. Dick quickly established an efficient operation, and was then sent to Hopewell, Virginia to accomplish the same mission at Du Pont's guncotton plant under construction there.

The photographer's next assignment was to make monthly panoramic photographs of construction progress at the various munitions plants. These were sent to the Engineering Department in Wilmington to add more impact to the regular progress reports submitted by the field engineers. Another reason for this work was to document visually the speed with which the plants were constructed.

The panoramic photographs, as long as fourteen feet, were taken on a Cirkut camera capable of making a 360° photograph. Powered by a key-wound-spring, a system of gears turned the camera around on top of a tripod while a roll of film, up to sixteen inches wide, moved past an open shutter. In order to get the views needed, Dick often took his large equipment to roof tops or up on scaffolding. It was only during the last few years of his career that he wore a safety harness, and then it was against his wishes. The Cirkut camera used by John A. Dick is in Hagley's collections, given by him in 1971.

The armistice of 1918 brought an immediate end to work on and in the munitions plants. John Dick dramatically recorded the post-war changes with a photograph showing approximately 3,000 of the 12,500 persons being paid and laid off in five hours at Old Hickory, Tennessee.

John Dick was next assigned to the Chemical Division's Eastern Laboratory at Gibbstown, New Jersey in 1919. Photography was by that time playing an

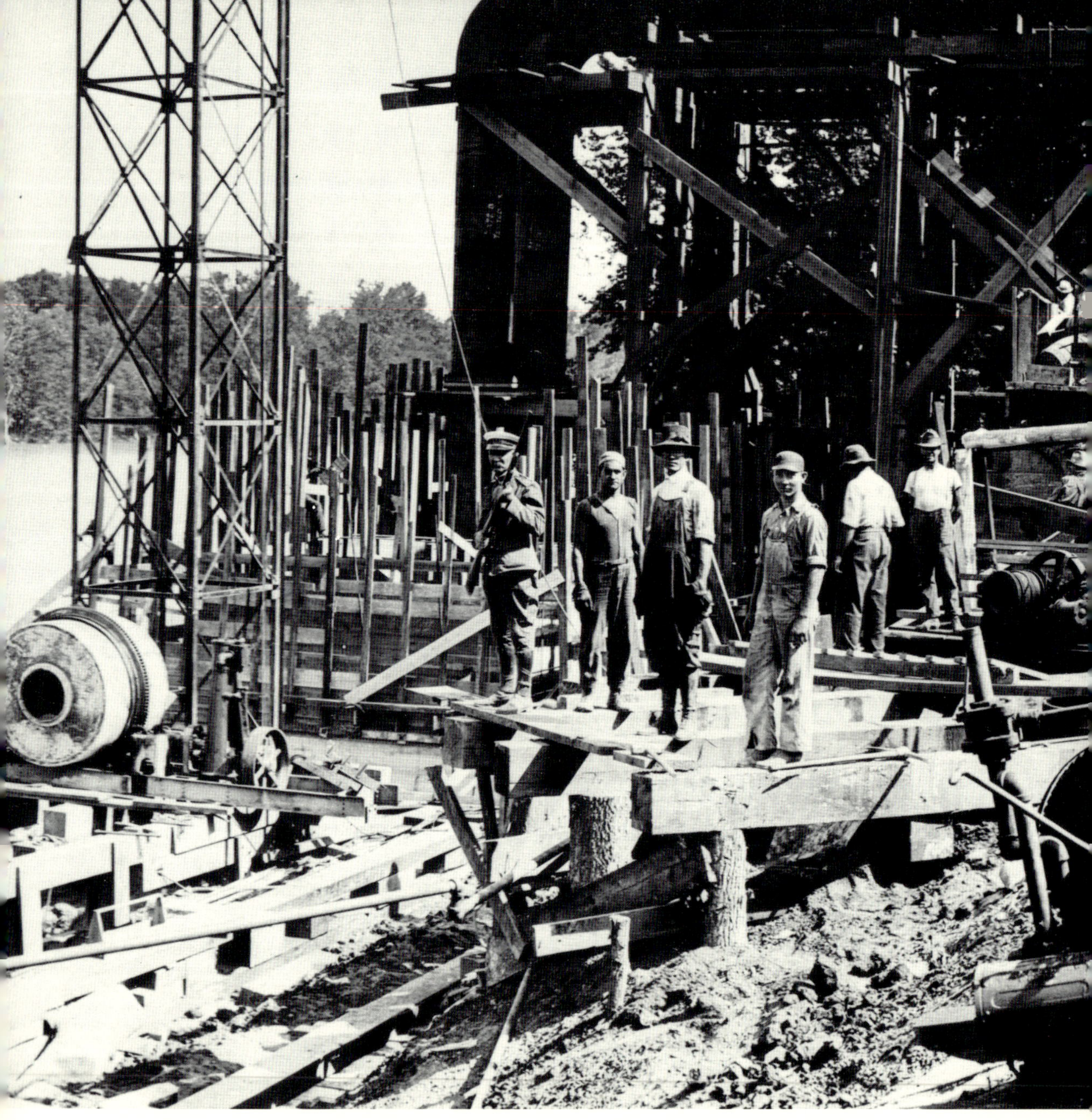

Detail from Cirkut print of Pump House construction at Old
Hickory plant, photographed by John A. Dick, July 6, 1918.

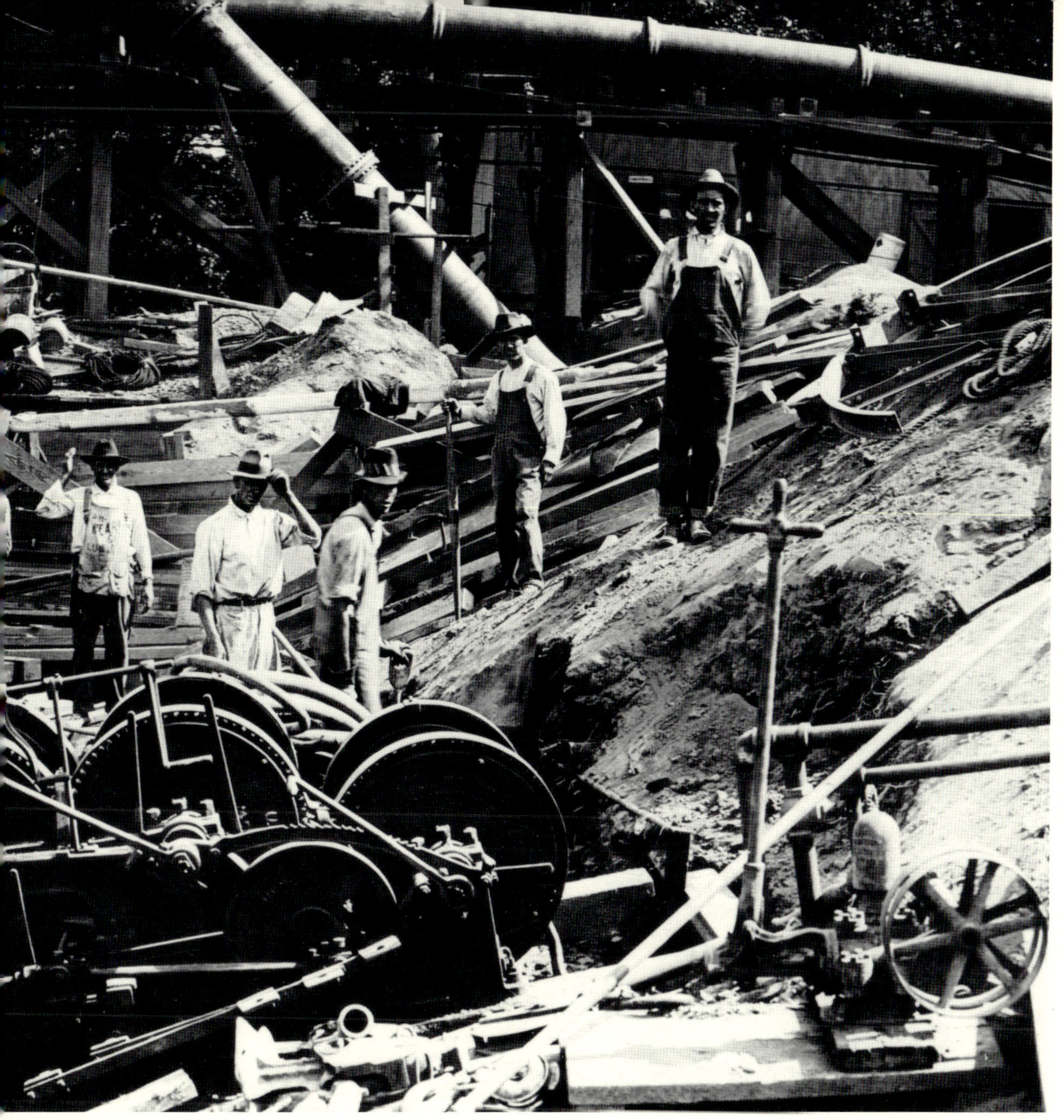

important role in product development and testing, and his technical skills were extensively used. In 1928 he was transferred to Wilmington to organize the first Photographic Studio at the Du Pont Company headquarters. In addition to planning and implementing a new activity, he continued as an active photographer himself. His work ranged from quarry blasts to experimental machinery to executive portraits. It was later said that he took photographs "of things animate and inanimate, articulate and inarticulate, organic and inorganic, animal, vegetable and mineral."[12]

This work continued until 1940 when the Engineering Department was once again rapidly building several defense plants. John Dick and his Cirkut camera again went on the road to make monthly record photographs of the construction progress. He regularly traveled to West Virginia, Tennessee, Kentucky, Indiana, Illinois, Minnesota, and Oklahoma. It took nearly a month to complete each round of coverage, keeping him on the road most of the time. He retired in 1944, as work on the Hanford Engineer Works' atomic plant in Washington state was

Street sweepers at Old Hickory plant, photographed by John A. Dick, January 16, 1919.

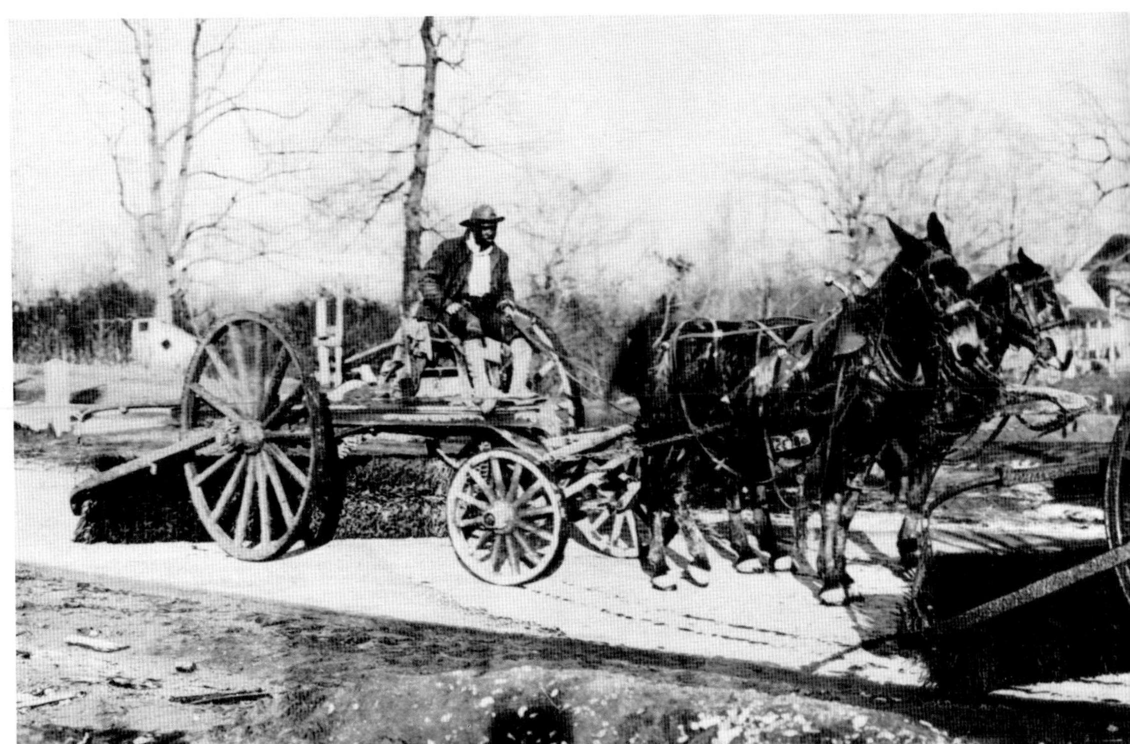

under way. While many Du Pont workers knew that there was some war-related construction in the pacific Northwest, they did not know what it was, as reflected in the following passage from his retirement booklet. "Finally, duty led him across the broad expanse of the continent to the shores of the Pacific, there to record on film the construction of that mystical plant whose very existence is shrouded in secrecy."[13]

The largest collection of John Dick's work which exists today is from the World War I construction projects. When the Du Pont Company closed its original Eleutherian Mills and Hagley powder yards along the Brandywine north of Wilmington in 1921, John Dick took a Cirkut print of the old mills, and it has become a frequently used photograph at Hagley. While some of his portrait and industrial work from between the wars is known, much of his work from that period is probably in different collections, unidentified, as is often the case with industrial photography.

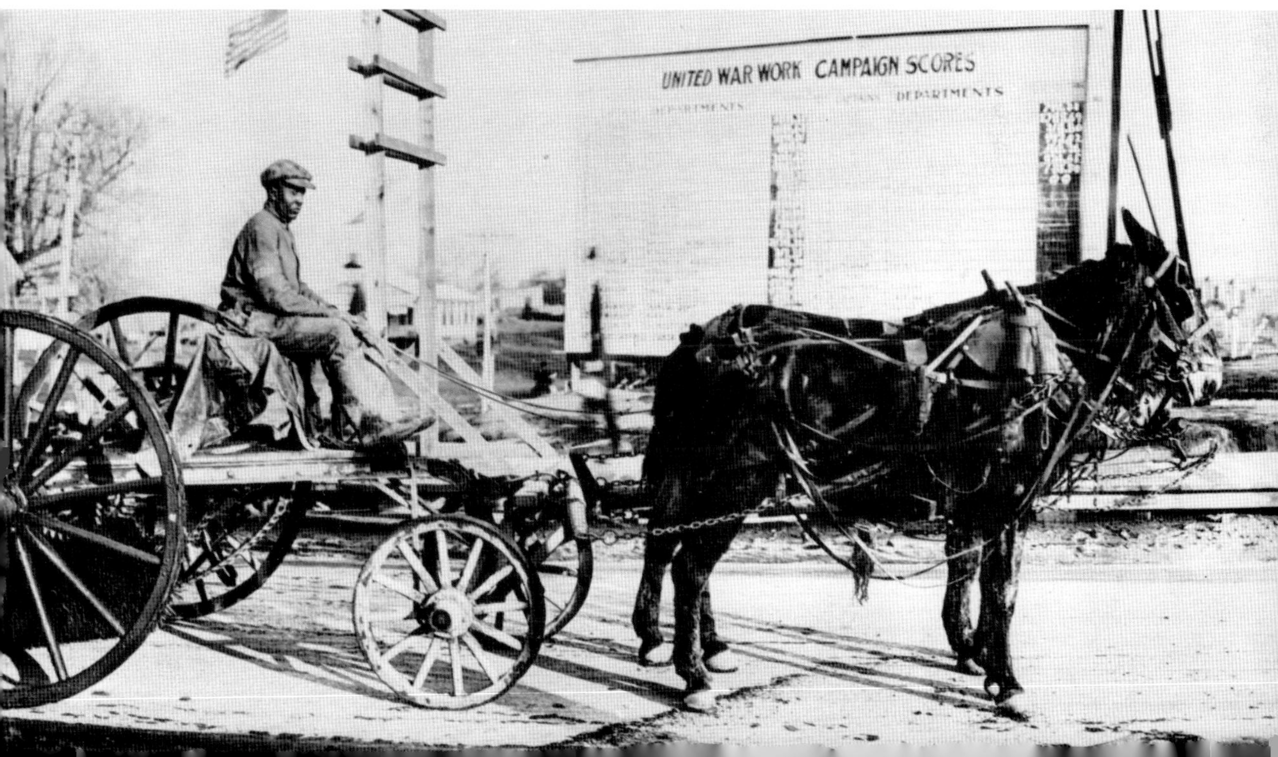

# THE DU PONT MAGAZINE · JANUARY 1931

# Industrial Photography As Fine Art

ONE continuing means of presenting a corporate image was through the executive portrait, which came to be a very elaborate art in the twentieth century. As the new century dawned, portrait photography was still tied to the traditions of the carte-de-visite and cabinet card photograph, i.e., portraits were straightforward documentary studio shots generally of ½ or ¼ length, usually showing little of the character of the sitter. Some firms specialized in executive portrait work and developed reputations based more on patronage and fashion than on artistic merit. Local photographers were often just as capable as some of these studios, yet executives still traveled to New York or Washington to have their portraits done.

By the 1920s, the art of portrait photography was changing as photographers attempted to individualize each portrait in order to better reflect the character of the subject. Usually, this took the form of a soft focus or selective focus, a warm-tone paper, and a heavily retouched negative. Sometimes the results were atrocious, as if the sitter were floating in a pool of murky water. This style, fortunately, did not last long.

With the 1930s came a return to sharply focused portraiture, but with a new emphasis on informality. The supreme practitioner of the new style executive portrait was Yousuf Karsh. Many Du Pont executives went to his studios, where they were often shown in more natural surroundings, holding pipes or cigarettes, or even resting their heads in their hands, all of this portrayed in Karsh's superbly mastered technique.

Along with individual portraiture, the group photograph was a staple of company photography throughout the twentieth century. The earliest group photographs of Du Pont executives were taken at conventions and dinners, as the early Executive Committees and Boards did not have group portraits taken. It was not until 1919 that a photograph was taken of the entire executive committee of the company, and it was not until twenty years later that this was done on any regular basis.

By 1931, the cover of the *Du Pont Magazine* was reflecting the latest trends in photography and design. This picture shows a pressure still at the Gulf Refinery in Philadelphia.

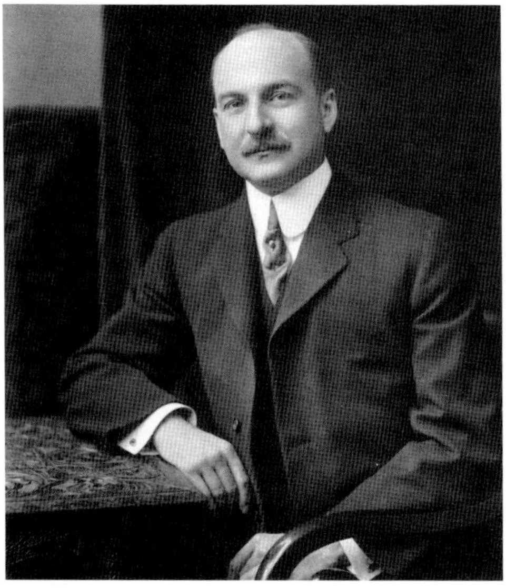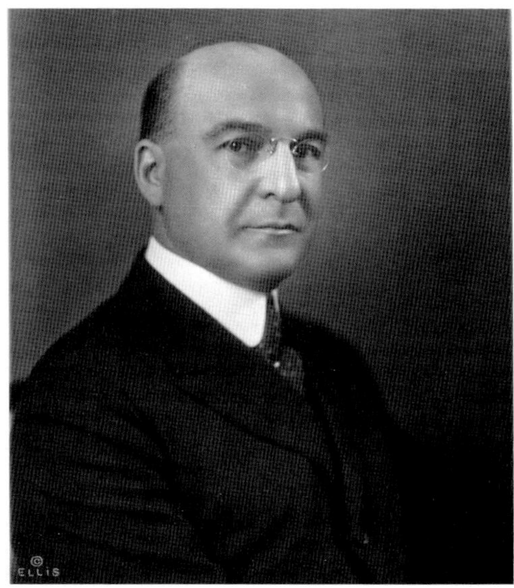

Two portraits of Pierre S. du Pont showing stylistic changes which took place from the time of the first (1917) to the second (1925).

The public in the nineteenth century often equated business with entrepreneurs, imagining, no doubt, a Rockefeller at his desk, or a J. P. Morgan running an empire from his New York office. With the rise of structured management in the twentieth century, however, the entrepreneur's place as a legitimate symbol of industry was diminished. At the same time, as Jack Hurley maintains, a "cult of the machine" was developing. Artists and photographers such as Paul Strand and Charles Sheeler began to examine the use of images from industries in their creations. Margaret Bourke-White, whose photography for *Fortune* magazine was widely admired, wrote that "to me these industrial forms were all the more beautiful because they were never designed to be beautiful. They had a simplicity of line that came from their direct application to a purpose. Industry, I felt, had evolved an unconscious beauty—often a hidden beauty that was waiting to be discovered. And recorded!" The details of machinery fascinated many photographers. Bourke-White declared further that "dynamos were more beautiful to me than pearls."[14] The need for a new image and the increasing interest of "art" with industrial themes led to new directions in the use of photography by businesses in the 1920s and 30s.

Gradually through the 1920s many companies, including Du Pont, turned from the "clear and sharp" straight documentary photographs desired previously to more "artistic" photographs taken from unusual angles and more contrasting light and dark areas. These were published first in countless company publications, such as monthly magazines and special booklets. The *Du Pont Magazine* followed this trend rather timidly at first, but with the appearance in 1930 of *Fortune* magazine, Du Pont began using the new style of photography more heavily. To do this, they turned to outside photographers, such as William S. Ellis of Wilmington and William M. Rittase of Philadelphia.

Rittase, one of the first to be hired, was commissioned to do photographs for the cover of *Du Pont Magazine*. He was very much in the mold of Paul Strand and Margaret Bourke-White, in that his style emphasized abstract patterns and "significant detail." His photograph of a sulfuric acid manufacturing facility at the Du Pont plant in Grasselli, New Jersey, shows a maze of pipes shot from an elevated position. No people appear and the picture tells very little about the process of making sulfuric acid. Instead, the pattern and the texture of the pipes is emphasized to create an eye-catching design and invite the reader to open the magazine to find out more. Occasionally Rittase over-exaggerated the abstract nature of a picture, as in his shot of smokeless powder pellets, sharply side lighted, and designed to be viewed upside down. Sometimes Rittase's work on the cover of *Du Pont Magazine* actually had nothing whatsoever to do with the company, such as the photograph used in January 1931, which was explained on the editorial page of that issue this way:

'Have you some interesting print of a subject that will typify the oil industry?' was asked.

'How about a derrick?' suggested Photographer Rittase, and while looking for one he came across the picture we have reproduced. This worm's-eye view of a pressure still with long lines of pipe extending upward seemed unusual enough to command attention. And because this number carries an article about pipe-line construction and how explosives figure in the work, we thought this print would meet our requirement as well as any. The picture was taken at the Gulf Refining Company's plant near Philadelphia.

Many of the stylistic details of these outside photographers hired by Du Pont were also used by local photographers called upon to produce standard publicity shots, making use of such devices as a "worm's-eye" angle in a 1953 photograph of a man washing his car. Again, the placement of the main subject diagonally within the picture was often a useful technical device for getting the maximum coverage of a subject, but it was also an artistic device characteristic of the period,

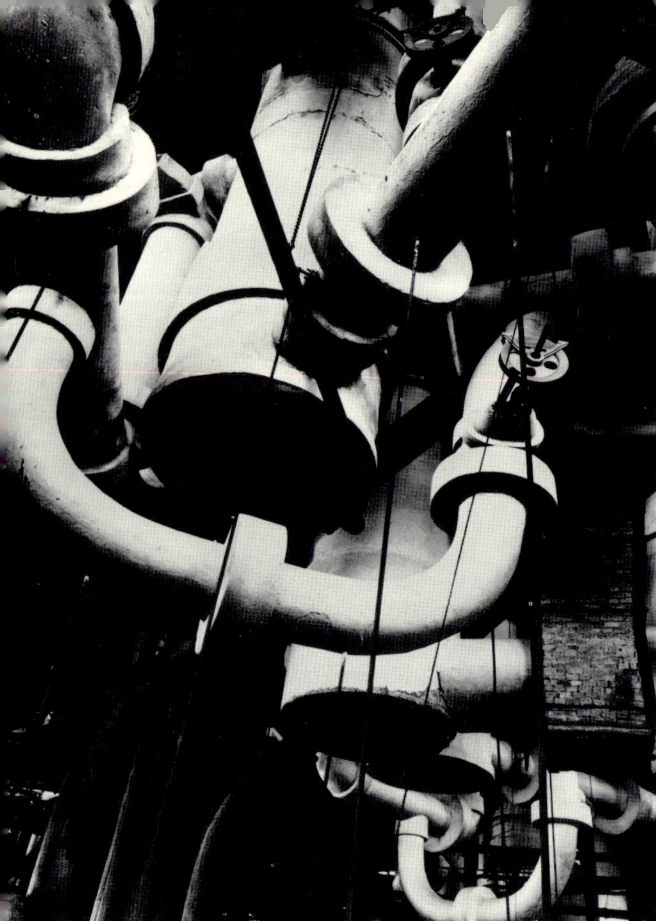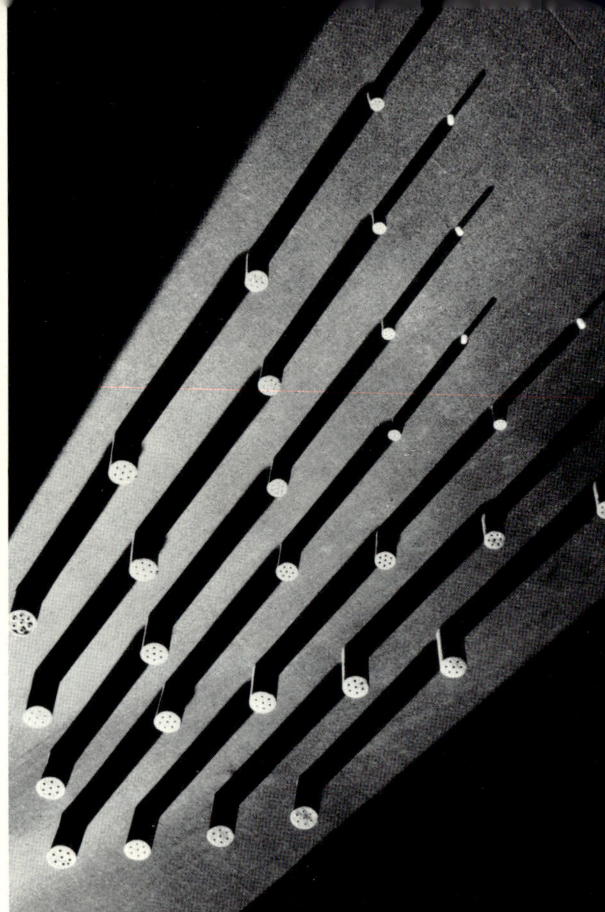

Above left: In the 1930s, the *Du Pont Magazine* frequently used the work of photographers from outside the company. This is a photograph by William Rittase of pipes at a Du Pont sulfuric acid plant, 1932.

Above right: Experimental pellets of smokeless gunpowder photographed by William Rittase in 1931.

Right: Inspecting cellulose sponge at the Buffalo, N.Y. plant of the Du Pont Company, c. 1935. Photographer unknown.

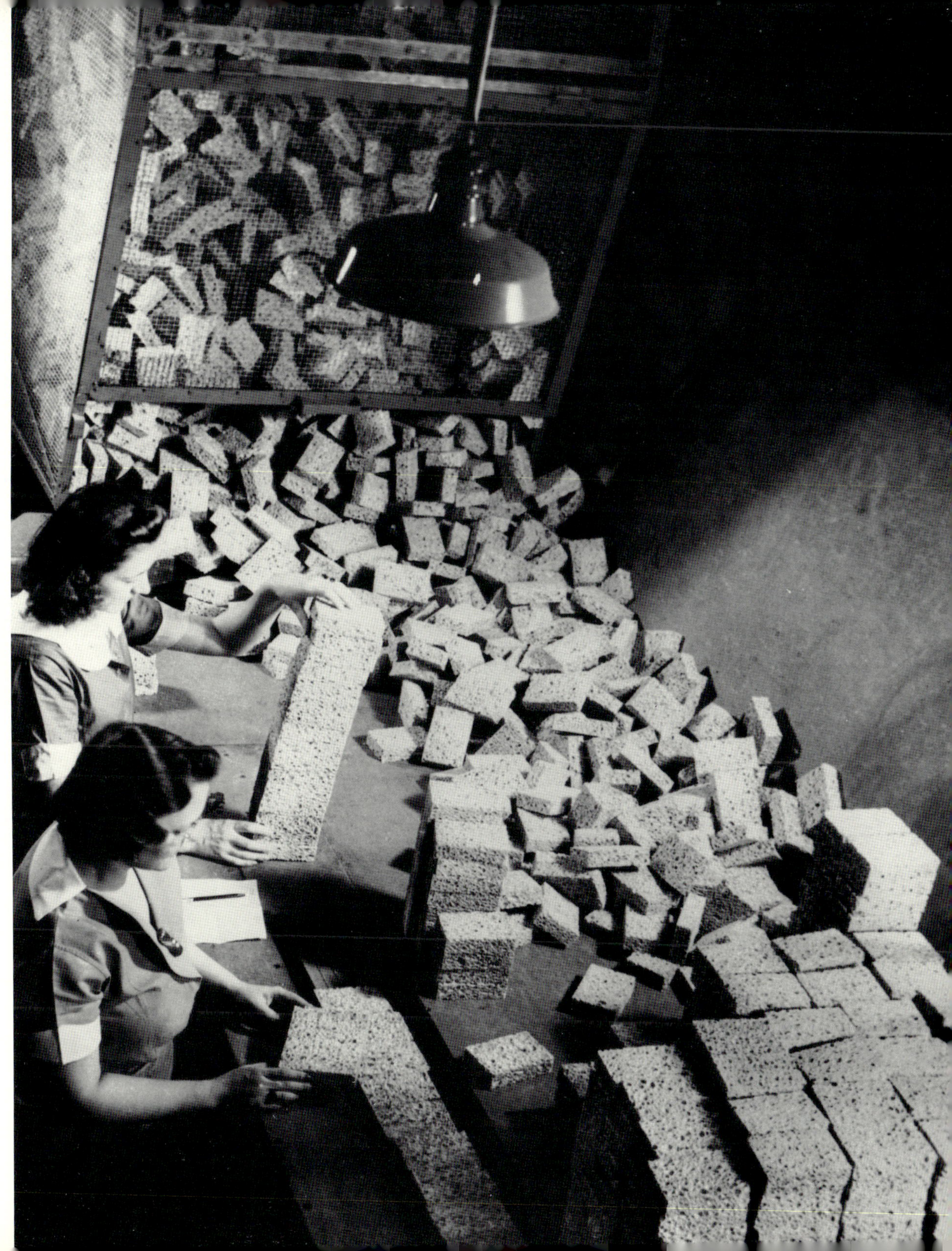

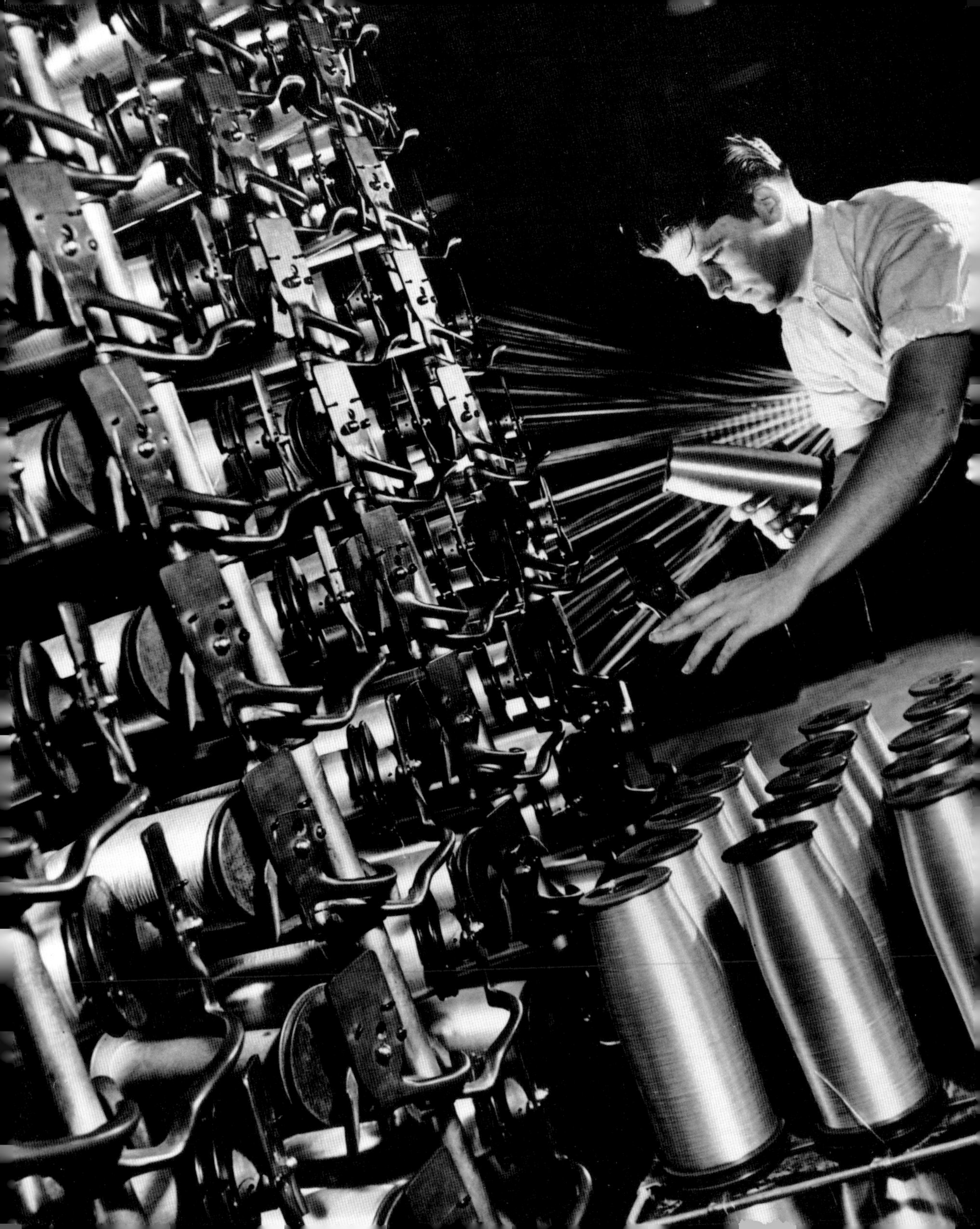

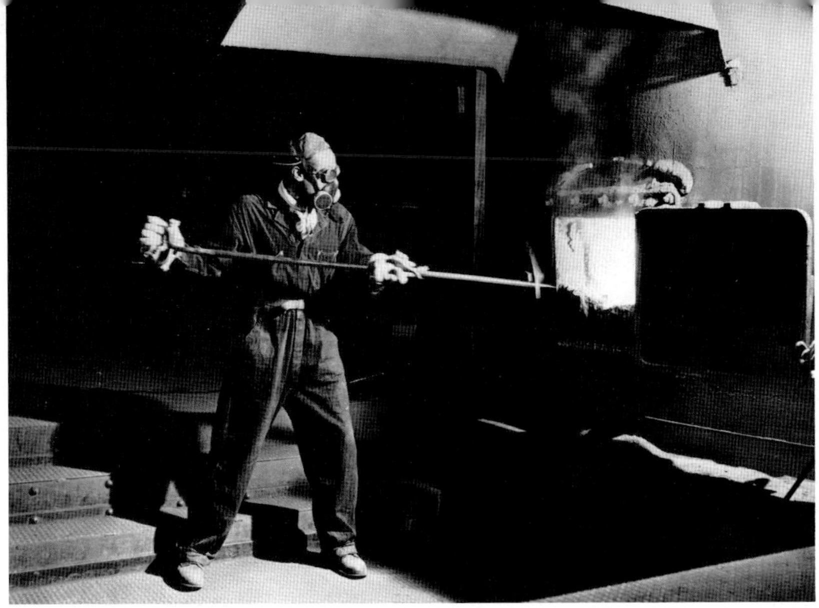



as in the photographs of workers inspecting man-made sponges at the Buffalo plant of the Du Pont Company.

Sometimes an anonymous photographer working for the Du Pont Company would produce a very striking image in the course of routine work, such as the view of an operator cleaning scale from a zinc roaster from a series of record shots on the making of sulfuric acid. This image is reminiscent of the work of the famous reformer and photographer Lewis Hine, and makes a vivid impression, despite its mundane purpose.

Robert Yarnall Richie was another outside photographer frequently used by the Du Pont Company. Richie's work dates mainly from the 1940s and was similar to Rittase's but often not as flamboyant. His picture of the production of synthetic fabrics at the Spruance Plant in Virginia illustrates this trait. Again the subject is placed at an angle within the frame of the picture, but it is not so harsh an angle as the pressure still in Rittase's earlier photograph. Richie involved more people in his photographs, perhaps as a result of a growing emphasis within the company on personnel relations.

In the years following World War II Du Pont added still more uses of photography with a personnel relations purpose. In the 1940s the firm began publication of *Better Living* magazine, which was to be for many years the major outlet for Du Pont Company photography.

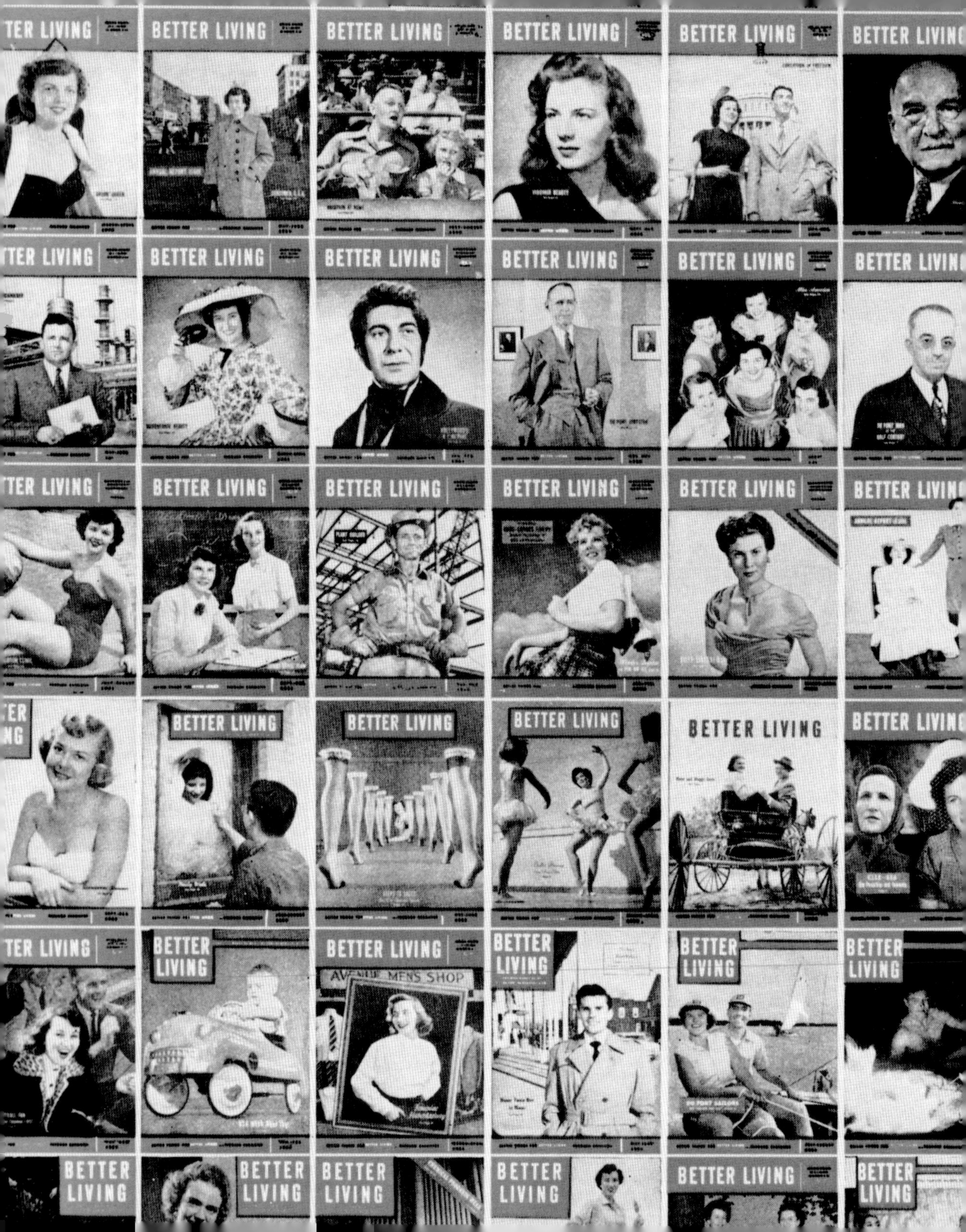

# Better Living

*BETTER LIVING* was a bi-monthly magazine for Du Pont Company employees, published from 1946 to 1972. A heavily illustrated journal with its own staff photographers, *Better Living* took its name from the firmly established Du Pont slogan "BETTER THINGS for BETTER LIVING . . . THROUGH CHEMISTRY." Several themes ran throughout the publication's twenty-six year existence, and like the contemporary commercial magazines *Life* and *Look*, virtually every article incorporated photographs to help tell, not just illustrate, the story.

In 1956 the Du Pont Company's Public Relations Department, which produced *Better Living,* issued a handbook called *Getting the Most From Your Plant Publication.* This was an effort to utilize better the forty-four individual Du Pont plant publications, and to encourage plants without publications to start them. The philosophy and objectives advocated for plant publications were the same as those practiced in *Better Living.* After stating that "What the employee knows, thinks and conveys has an important bearing on management's fate and the success of the enterprise," the handbook listed as the first objective "build[ing] esprit de corps, the sense of belonging and of participation in a common objective." *Better Living* never departed from that goal. Throughout its existence the magazine profiled scores of positions within the firm, literally everything from Accountant to Zoologist, including corporate executives, plant workers, secretaries and stockholders.

*Better Living* informed Du Pont workers that they indeed had a better living than they might have had if they were employed by a less caring corporation. It went on to show employees how their work led to a better living for others, particularly citizens of the United States, and why Du Pont's home country enjoyed a higher standard of living than any other nation. Another frequent theme was the burden of taxes on individuals and corporations, and the threat that they posed to the good living the Du Pont workers earned. *Better Living* very much reflected the post-war prosperity that many Americans enjoyed.

Workers in consumer goods industries could easily see how people benefited from their work. This was not the case, however, for most Du Pont employees, since the products of their labor went not directly to consumers, but rather to other industries. Therefore, an article on sulfuric acid showed not only the people, processes, and plants involved in its manufacture, but also photographs of consumer products that utilized sulfuric acid in their manufacture of items such as milk, refrigerators, and cellophane.

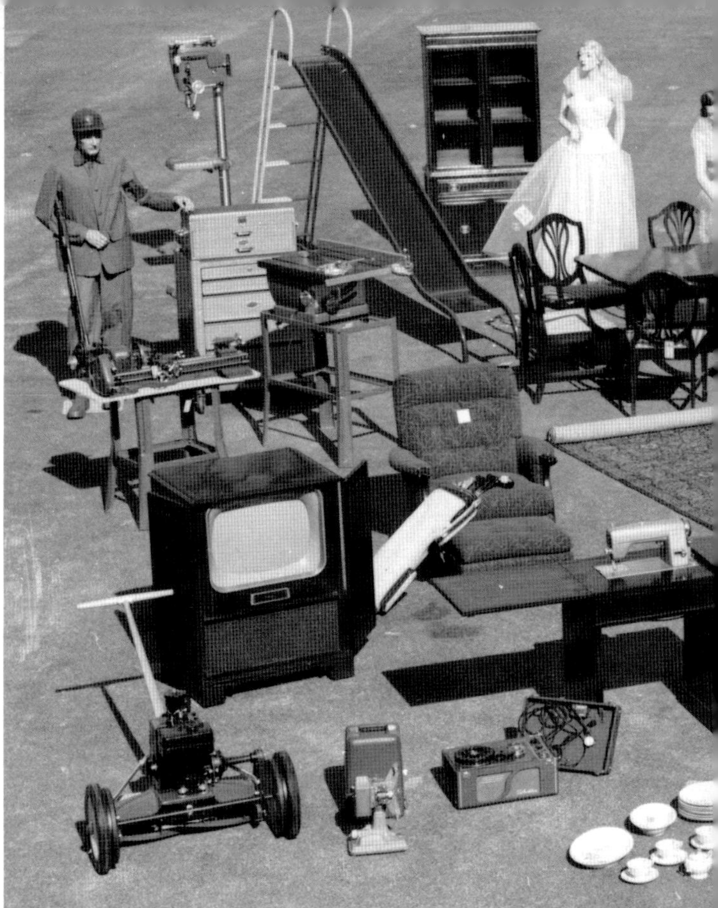

"Taxes Are Paid in Lost Dreams," published in May 1953, stated that the average Du Pont worker paid $7,000 in direct and indirect taxes from 1946 through 1952. A Du Pont family was to select $7,000 worth of merchandise from a department store, to show how its members would have spent that money themselves.

Staff photographer Alex Henderson went to great lengths to produce photographs with a vivid impact. One of the most memorable and widely reproduced of his photographs showed a family of four surrounded by all the food they would consume in a year. It was used to illustrate a 1951 article entitled "Why We Eat Better." Mr. Henderson spent many hours in a frozen food locker arranging and rearranging the food and people in his picture until he was satisfied. The article contained smaller prints of the photo with various amounts of food blocked out to show how much less food was available to similar families in several other countries. Articles in other *Better Living* issues pointed out Du Pont's contributions to agriculture as well as to food packaging and distribution.

Henderson's photograph of "Why We Eat Better" was carried in *Life* magazine, and it proved so effective and popular that it has been updated twice, with the most recent version issued as both poster and placemat. It also led to many

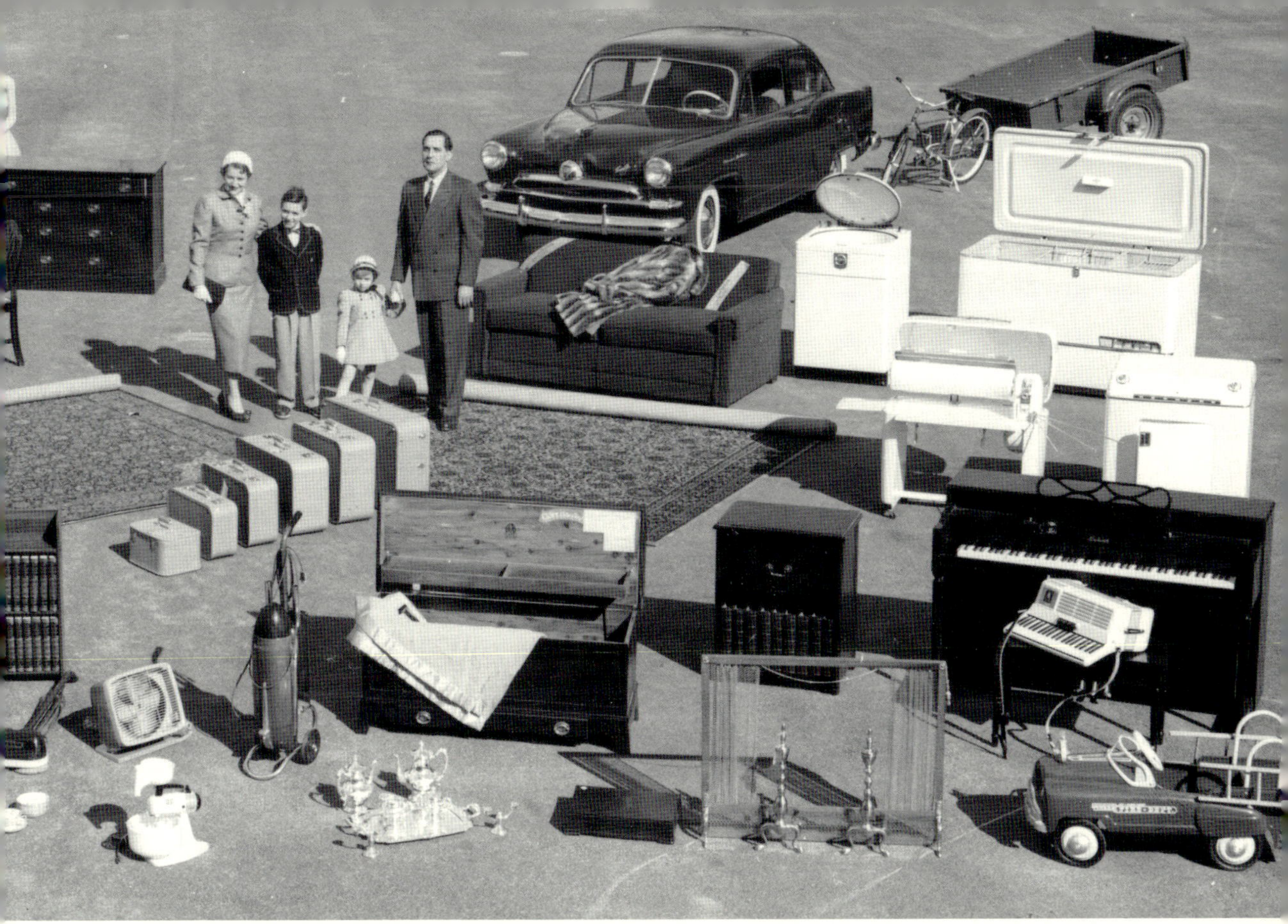

Glass blower.

Welder.

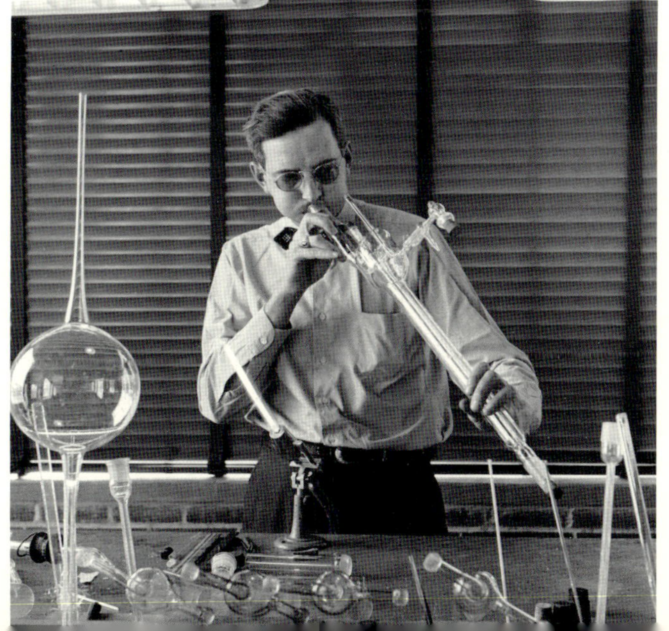

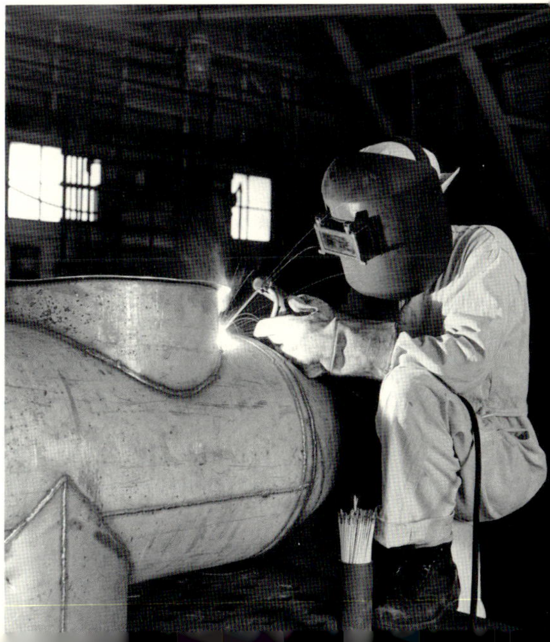

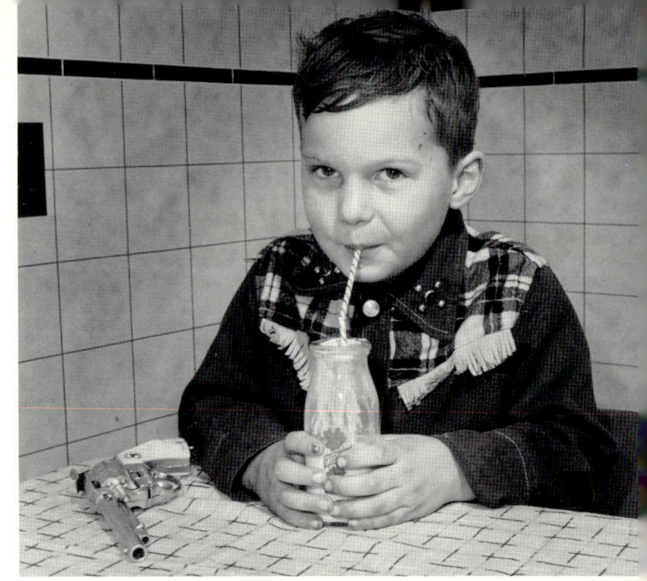

RIGHT: While most people never purchase sulfuric acid, each person in the United States indirectly uses over a quart of it per day. It is used for testing the butterfat content of milk.

BELOW: "Why We Eat Better," photographed by Alex Henderson for November 1951 issue of *Better Living*.

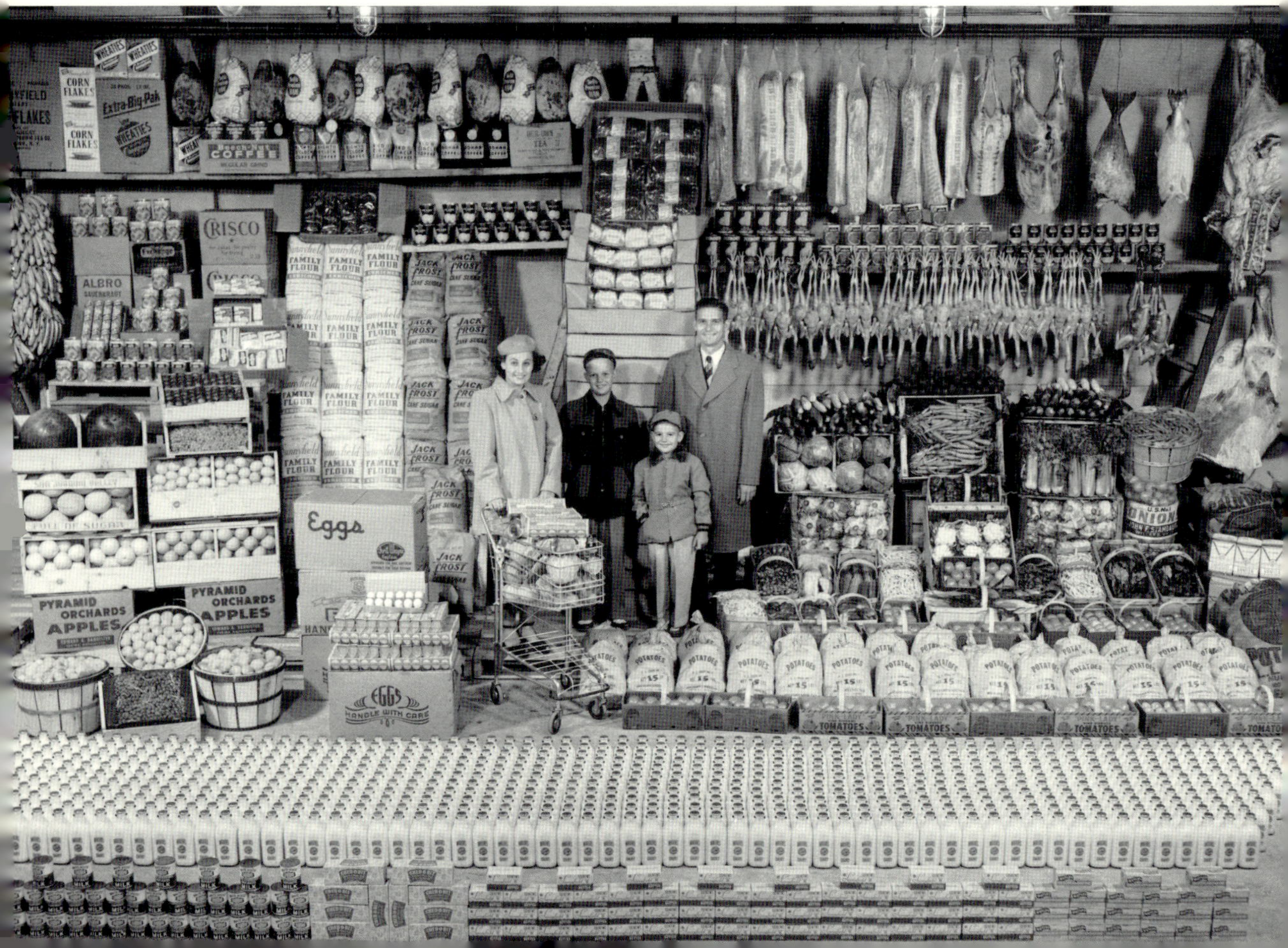

other photographs using the same format to make a variety of points, including Du Pont's commendable safety record, the variety of its products, the stability of its work force, the challenges of its research department, and the burden of taxation.

Through photography *Better Living* introduced Du Pont employees to company history, showed how easy the adjustment was for a family transferred from one location to another, pointed out what a good corporate citizen Du Pont was in the areas in which it had plants, acclaimed the basic, wholesome, down-to-earth lives of families connected with Du Pont, explored the changing role of women in the work force in the quarter century after World War II, proclaimed Du Pont's commitment to peace and contributions to defense, and held out the promise of an even better life ahead.

The handbook on *Getting the Most From Your Plant Publication* concluded that another

> major thing a publication can do for management is interpret the economic, social and political subjects of importance to the company. Over the years, all industrial people have been subjected to an endless barrage of misinformation and accusations—ranging from outright condemnation of business management and its motivations to confusing attacks on bigness and technology. Myths of exorbitant profits, of anti-social concentrations of power, of the exploited worker, of large business smashing small business—all have been systematically built.

Through the use of photojournalism, *Better Living* systematically attempted to correct the myths and misinformation to which top management felt Du Pont employees were being subjected.

*Better Living* became a model for other industrial employee magazines. William C. Halley, who served on the editorial staffs of both *Better Living* and *Du Pont Magazine*, wrote the 1959 Chilton book, *Employee Publications: Theory and Practice of Communications in the Modern Organization.* Many of his examples of what constituted a good publication came from *Better Living,* and his four objectives for a "thoughtful organization periodical" were a basic outline of the Du Pont publication.[15]

Alex Henderson became a staff photographer shortly after the creation of *Better Living,* and served until the magazine ceased publication in 1972. Other staff photographers were John Alexander in the early years, followed by Howard Slater. Photographs from 910 articles published during the twenty-six years of *Better Living* are in the Hagley collections. In most instances these include negatives and proofs from an entire project, not just the frames selected for publication.

RIGHT: Automobile suspended
by Mylar film.

BELOW: Machinery for inserting
bristles in toothbrush handles, one
of Du Pont's consumer products.

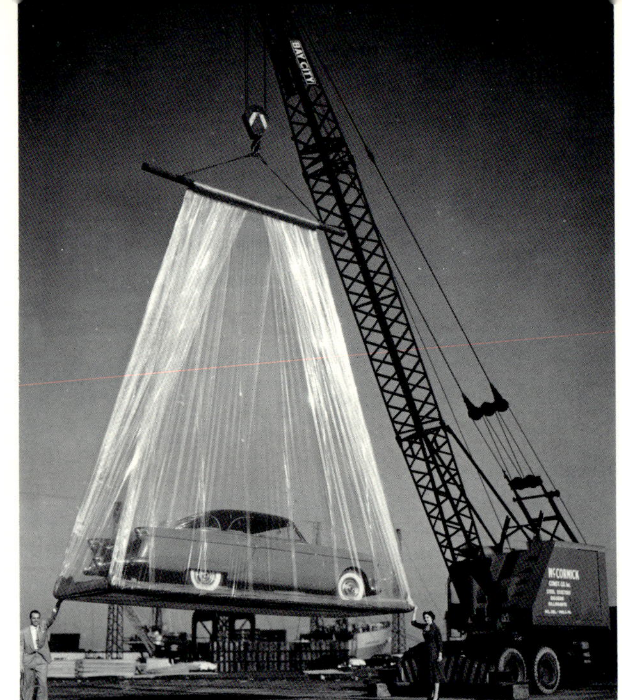

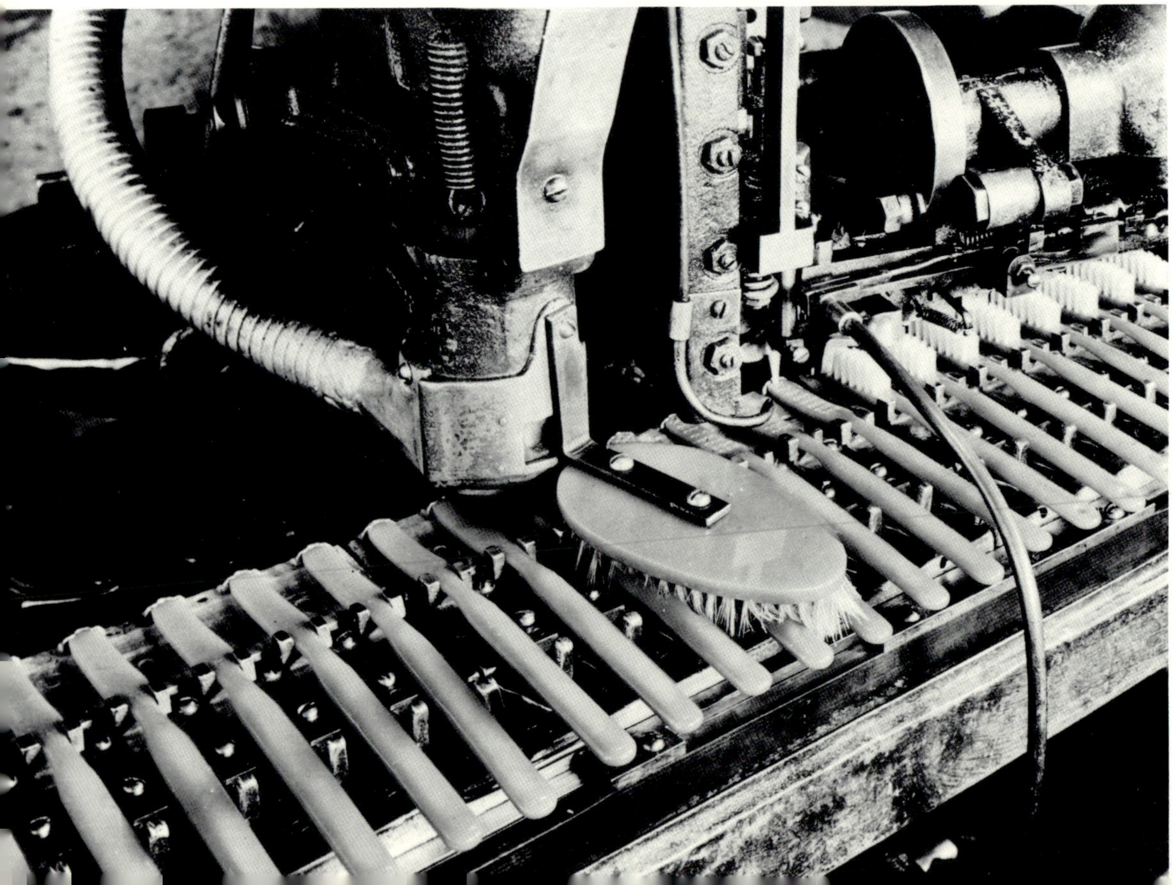

Much of the work generated for *Better Living* was reused in a separate publication from the Public Relations Department, *This Is Du Pont*. While the former magazine was aimed at the Du Pont employee, *This Is Du Pont* repackaged not only existing photographs, but often entire articles, to tell the outside world more about the Du Pont Company.

In 1952 the Du Pont Company organized a Product Information section within the Public Relations Department. Its main purpose was to create news releases accompanied by photographs, which would be run editorially by trade journals and newspapers, in effect creating inexpensive publicity and indirect advertising. To be used, the news releases had to include genuinely interesting information about a Du Pont product, its development, manufacture, or applications. They could not be direct commercial promotions of a product itself, that being the proper work of the Advertising Department.

Public Relations staff members in Product Information were assigned to specific operating departments, and they reported jointly to the heads of PR and the specific department. They were responsible for selecting themes, writing the news releases, and having the needed photographs produced. There were no staff photographers assigned to the program but rather the Product Information officer hired photographers for the individual jobs. These may have been "hired" from Du Pont's Photo Studio, or from the outside commercial field. The Product Information files ended up with only those finished photographs selected for use, not negatives and proofs of everything shot, as was the case with *Better Living*. The Product Information files acquired by Hagley in 1973 include more than 4,000 photo prints, mostly with explanatory captions.

While *Better Living* was an example of photo journalism, Product Information relied more on the single striking photograph which would immediately attract attention and lead the reader to the caption and article to find out what it was all about. The photograph was an integral part of the package, but not an end in itself.

Product Information photographs and their news releases told what Du Pont did, sometimes how it was done, and why that was important to a reader. They went for the dramatic where possible, such as photographing an automobile suspended by straps of Mylar film. More often, however, the photographs were more in the "Gee Whiz" nature of "what is that?" or "what is he doing?" Occasionally photographs taken for *Better Living* or Product Information would be used by the other, but generally not. Even though the Product Information section was not organized until 1952, some of the photographs are from World War II, when that kind of promotional work was done under different auspices.

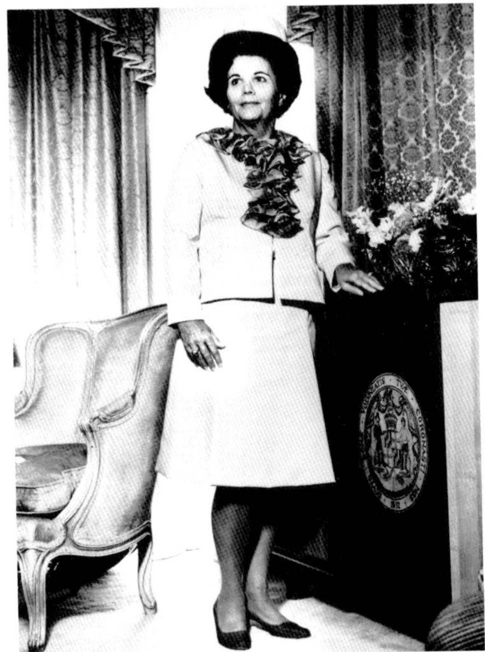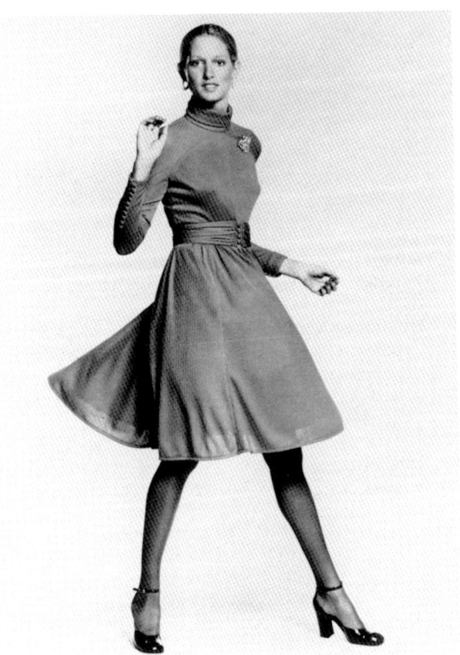





Product Information for Textile Fibers was handled out of that department's offices in New York City's Empire State Building. Their photo records comprise Hagley's most recent Du Pont Company collection. These too were issued with press releases for editorial use, designed to establish and strengthen in the reader's mind the connection between Du Pont, maker of fibers, and the garment and fashion industry.

The historic photograph collections of the Hagley Museum and Library have grown and evolved, as has the Du Pont Company's use of photography. At Hagley we formally recognized photographs as primary source material in 1968 by creating a separate department responsible for their collection, care, and use. This booklet is but a sample of the riches in our entire pictorial holdings, and our collections in the area of photographic documentation continue to expand. Scholars use more than 100,000 of these images each year in pursuit of a wide variety of topics. We anticipate issuing similar guides to other collections in the future.

# FOOTNOTES

[1]Although most members of the du Pont family spell their name with a lower case d, the official company policy is to use a capital in its name, i.e., the Du Pont Company.

[2]There are no known photographs of the powder yards from the particular angle that Otis and Dalmas painted them. Although photography appeared after their work, no one thought to take their paintings as models and reproduce them photographically. This might be due, in part, to the heavily wooded nature of the site from which they were sketched, and that it was private property closed to visitors after the Civil War.

[3]F. Jack Hurley, *Industry and the Photographic Image* (New York: George Eastman House, Rochester, in association with Dover Publications, Inc., 1980), p. 1.

[4]One example was "Beautiful in Death," a photograph that features one of the photographer's assistants lying awkwardly among some large rocks, trying to capitalize on a standard Civil War view of the dead. The assistant shows up very much alive in pictures later in the series.

[5]William S. Dutton, *Du Pont: One Hundred and Forty Years* (New York: Charles Scribner's Sons, 1949), p. 150.

[6]All three brothers went to school in Massachusetts, and their correspondence contains many references to photography. For example, in 1891 Henry Belin du Pont wrote to his mother that "I have been out walking all afternoon with La Motte. We took our cameras along and snapped them on people. We had great fun snapping them on girls over on Commonwealth Avenue. We tried to get some pretty ones but they were few and far between. I am going to develop them this evening."

[7]See, for example, Dutton, *Du Pont*, p. 169 ff., and Alfred D. Chandler, Jr. and Stephen Salsbury, *Pierre S. du Pont and the Making of the Modern Corporation* (New York: Harper & Row, 1971), Chapter 3.

[8]Brian Coe and Paul Gates, *The Snapshot Photograph: the Rise of Popular Photography, 1888–1939* (London: Ash & Grant Ltd., 1977), p. 12.

[9]Hurley, *Industry and the Photographic Image*, p. 46.

[10]Dutton, *Du Pont*, p. 173.

[11]Chandler and Salsbury, *Pierre S. du Pont*, p. xxi.

[12]"John A. Dick: His Du Pont Company Career, 1915–1944." A Photocopy of this unpublished document is in the Pictorial Collections and Audio Visual Services Department at Hagley.

[13]ibid.

[14]Margaret Bourke-White, *Portrait of Myself* (New York: Simon and Schuster, 1963), pp. 40, 49.

[15]References have been made above to *Du Pont Magazine*, a publication of the Advertising (now Marketing Communications) Department, which began in 1913 and is still in publication. While it has been heavily illustrated almost from the beginning, it is primarily a consumer rather than producer of photographs. *Du Pont Magazine* depicts ways in which other businesses use Du Pont intermediate products to produce, package and market their end products. Therefore, most of the photography included in it is from those other firms illustrating their operations. The Hagley Museum and Library has a complete run of *Du Pont Magazine*, but has no photo collections relating to it.

# Checklist of Du Pont Company Photographs in the Hagley Museum and Library

THE history of the Du Pont Company is a very complex one, especially in the twentieth century, when the company expanded tremendously. Good summary chronologies of the company's history are published in J. B. Riggs, *A Guide to the Manuscripts in the Eleutherian Mills Historical Library*, Greenville, Delaware, 1970, and its supplement published in 1978. The supplement also contains a comprehensive list of companies absorbed by Du Pont.

The more than 80,000 photographs of the Du Pont Company housed in the Hagley Museum and Library have come in over a period of many years, and consequently are contained in many different accessions. Complete finding aids to these accessions are available in the Pictorial Collections and Audio-Visual Services Department. What follows is a checklist of the larger collections. Not listed are collections containing only du Pont family material, or artwork, posters, and the like. The pictures, of course, are only part of a much larger collection of Du Pont Company materials in the Hagley Museum and Library, which also includes imprints, manuscripts, and artifacts.

# CONTENTS

## Accession #84.207

**ADVERTISING DEPARTMENT COLLECTION**

## 273 items

## 1898–1950

Miscellaneous photographs used by the Advertising Department, including plant views (mostly explosives plants), personnel (including many Eastern Lab and early chemists), miscellaneous pictures used in Arthur P. Van Gelder and Hugo Schlatter, *History of the Explosives Industry in America* (New York: Columbia University Press, 1927), and views of the "S.S. Ethyl" bromine recovery ship (1925).

## Accessions #71.MSS.380, 71.MSS.876, 72.270, 73.278

**ATLANTIC CITY, NEW JERSEY EXHIBIT**

## 5,856 items

## 1916–1957

Photographs of displays at the Du Pont Company's Atlantic City, New Jersey, exhibit building on the boardwalk. These show consumer goods using Du Pont products, and the displays were changed monthly. Some views of people on the Boardwalk and viewing the exhibits. 72.270 also contains views of exhibits in Wilmington office buildings.

See also 68.1.59.G.21.

## Accession #72.341 Part II

*BETTER LIVING* **MAGAZINE PICTURE FILE**

## c. 36,000 items

## 1946–1972

Photographs used in production of Du Pont Company's *Better Living* magazine, published by the Public Relations Department for company employees. Pictures cover all aspects of Du Pont Company activities, as well as depicting the quality of American life in the post-war period. Includes alternate versions of photographs from those actually used in the magazine, mostly as negatives with contact prints. Pictures are filed under the name of the article they appeared in, and there is a chronological index to titles. There is also a general file of plant views. Most pictures are black and white, although there is some color photography in the later years.

Accessions #70.220, 71.331., 71.MSS.501, 71.MSS.504, 72.233, 73.303, 73.342, 73.350, 73.355

**CARNEY'S POINT, NEW JERSEY PLANT COLLECTION**

127 items

c. 1890–1920

Photographs of Carney's Point, N.J. smokeless powder plant facilities and employees, including aftermaths of fires and explosions, guards during Spanish-American War, and employee identification portraits.

Accession #72.422

**CENTRAL SYSTEMS AND SERVICES DEPARTMENT PICTURE FILE**

651 items

1888–1954

Photographs of exteriors and interiors of Du Pont Building, Wilmington, Delaware, including Hotel du Pont, the Playhouse, and the Wilmington Trust Company; Nemours Building, Wilmington, Delaware; Louviers Engineering Building, near Newark, Delaware. Also included are views of Wilmington in vicinity of Du Pont Building both before and after construction of the same.

Accession #74.213

**JASPER CRANE (1881–1961) COLLECTION**

c. 255 items

1930–1967

Many personal photographs, but includes photo album of trip that Crane (Du Pont Company vice-president and director) made to South America (c. 1930), and portraits of Du Pont Company executives and Board of Directors.

Accessions 69.138 through 69.191

**PANORAMIC PHOTOGRAPHS BY JOHN A. DICK**

163 items

1915–c. 1945

Panoramic photographs of various Du Pont Company sites taken by John A. Dick, company photographer. Includes the following sites in New Jersey: Carney's Point, Deepwater (Chamber's Works), Haskell, Parlin, Penniman, Pompton Lakes, and Repauno. Also includes the Experimental Station; Louviers, Colorado; Spruance plant in Richmond, Virginia; Hopewell, Virginia; Old Hickory, Tennessee; and miscellaneous others. Some views of employees and conventions.

See also 68.1.G54 (especially for many more Old Hickory panoramics) and 82.300.

## Accession 72.238

**EDMOND RHETT DU PONT COLLECTION OF FRANCIS G. DU PONT PHOTOGRAPHY**

292 items

c. 1890–1920

Photographs of the Du Pont powder mills on the Brandywine and at Carney's Point, New Jersey. Also, unidentified powder mill and photographs of F. G. du Pont and family.

## Accession #71.424

**HENRY BELIN DU PONT (1873–1902) COLLECTION**

323 items

c. 1890–1910

Many personal photographs of family, friends, and travels, but also contains views of the powder yards on the Brandywine and surrounding area, including Louviers.

## Accession #73.399

**JAMES Q. DU PONT COLLECTION**

85 items

c. 1940–1970

Photographs relating to activities of James Q. du Pont (1902–1973), Administrative assistant in the Du Pont Company's Public Relations Department. Includes views of Seaford, Delaware nylon plant, and Chambers Works at Deepwater, N.J.

## Accessions #69.2, 69.119, 76,341, 77.240, no number

**CONSTRUCTION OF DU PONT BUILDING, WILMINGTON, DELAWARE**

389 items

1905–1969

Photographs of construction of the Du Pont Building (company headquarters), Wilmington, Delaware. The first section was begun in 1905. Also includes views of Nemours Building and construction of Brandywine Building (1969).

See also 82.300 Engineering Department Collection, 72.422 Central Systems & Services Department Collection, and 68.1.G54.1.559.

## Accession #68.1.G54

**DU PONT MUSEUM COLLECTION**

4,430 items

1885–1952

Photographs of Du Pont Company and absorbed companies compiled by the Du Pont Company Museum and transferred to the Hagley Museum in 1954. Includes views of executives and staff, groups at meetings and dinners, early offices, Du Pont Building, Carney's Point plant, Repauno plant, Eastern Laboratory, Experimental Station, many other miscellaneous sites, aftermaths of explosions at plants (most pre-WWI), construction, WWI expansion construction (many panoramic photographs), some photographs used in Van Gelder and Schlatter, *History of the Explosives Industry,* and post WWI plant construction.

Most of the pictures date from 1900 to 1930.

## Accession #84.226

*DU PONT: THE AUTOBIOGRAPHY OF AN AMERICAN ENTERPRISE* **PICTURE FILE**

345 items

c. 1865–1952

Photographs (mostly copy photos) used in the production of *Du Pont: The Autobiography of an American Enterprise,* published by E. I. du Pont de Nemours & Co., and distributed by Charles Scribner's Sons, New York in 1952.

Many of the original pictures used in this 150th Anniversary book were returned to their owners and are not in this file. Many of the pictures are heavily retouched.

## Accession #82.300

**ENGINEERING DEPARTMENT PICTURE FILE**

c. 16,000 items

1905–1950

Photographs of on-site construction and structures by Du Pont Company field engineers from 192 different company sites. Most of the pictures are snapshot photographs by the engineers themselves, although there are also panoramic photographs and prints by professional photographers. Included are some 8 × 10 black and white photographs of the various construction stages of the Du Pont Building in Wilmington.

## Accession #84.227

**ENGINEERING MISSION TO FRANCE**

471 items

1928

Photographs of French acetate industry taken by unidentified Du Pont Company photographer, titled "Engineering Mission in 1928."

Accessions 71.MSS.921, 77.242, 82.304
**EXHIBITS AT WORLD'S FAIR AND EXPOSITIONS**
180 items
1939–1953

Photographs of company exhibits at New York World's Fairs, 1939 and 1964, San Francisco Golden Gate Exposition, 1939, Argentina, 1941, and small traveling exhibits, 1953.

Accessions #70.56, 70.57, 71.MSS.926
**EXPLOSIVES DELIVERY TRUCKS**
1,040 items
c. 1910–1960

Photographs of Du Pont Company explosives delivery trucks, also includes some views of explosives ships.
See also 68.1.G54.1.116

Accession #70.1
**PIERRE GENTIEU COLLECTION**
c. 350 items
1883–1917

Photographs by Pierre Gentieu (powder yard worker) of Du Pont powder mills on the Brandywine, employees, employees' families and housing, and du Pont family homes.
N.B. The original negatives for these photographs are housed at the library of the Historical Society of Delaware. The Hagley Museum and Library has a set of prints made from these negatives in the 1940s.

Accession #74.389
**HANFORD ENGINEER WORKS COLLECTION**
268 items
1943–1945

Three albums of photographs from Hanford, including "Photographic History, Medical Division, 1943–1945," "Hanford Yuletide Carnival . . . Dec. 18, 1943," and "1944 H.E.W. Safety Exposition." Hanford was built during World War II to manufacture plutonium for the atomic bomb.

## Accession #68.7

**HARRINGTON—SCHIFF COLLECTION**

## 673 items

## 1889–c. 1915

Personal photographs of Edward M. Harrington, manager of the Aetna Dynamite Works, Aetna, Indiana, and later an efficiency expert for the Du Pont Company. Photographs are mostly of Aetna works, but also some miscellaneous Du Pont sites including 1903 survey of properties.

## Accessions #69.143, 72.384

**INDIANA ORDNANCE WORKS COLLECTION**

## 762 items

## 1940–1941

Photographs showing construction of the Indiana Ordnance Works, Charlestown, Indiana. Includes illustrated monthly progress reports.
    See also 84.207, 72.341 (Box 6, explosives) and 68.1.G54.1.185 & .195 (panoramic photographs.)

## Accession #69.85

**MRS. CAZENOVE G. LEE, JR (MARGUERITE DU PONT LEE) COLLECTION**

## 131 items

## c. 1900–1930

Mostly snapshot photographs of Brandywine area, including Du Pont Powder yards, and miscellaneous Du Pont Company plants. Also includes personal photographs of Cazenove G. Lee, Jr. (1882–1945).

## Accessions #71.MSS.863, 71.MSS.1028, no number

**150TH ANNIVERSARY CELEBRATION**

## 833 items

## July & August 1952

Photographs of celebration at original site of Du Pont powder mills (Eleutherian Mills) in honor of the 150th anniversary of the company, showing both the rehearsal and the actual ceremony on the following day. Includes the Luther D. Reed (Du Pont Company executive) collection.

## Accession #74.288
*PACKAGES AND PEOPLE* **MAGAZINE PICTURE FILE**
## 81 items
## c. 1960

Photographs used in Du Pont Company's Film Department's periodical, "Packages and People." Positive microfilm.

## Accession #84.225
**PUBLIC AFFAIRS DEPARTMENT COLLECTION**
## 3,050 items
## c. 1830–1975

Part I—Photographs of Du Pont Company executives (mostly 1930–1970) including company presidents, "deceased" file, and executive groups.

Part II—Du Pont International activities, c. 1960–1967, including views in Europe, Scandinavia, South America, and Japan. Color slides.

Part III—Various plants and sites, filed by company department, c. 1945–1970.

## Accession #72.341 Part I
**PUBLIC RELATIONS DEPARTMENT**
**PRODUCT INFORMATION SECTION PICTURE FILE**
## 4,494 items
## 1916–1968

Photographs covering many Du Pont facilities and activities, including industrial processes as well as finished products. The collection is divided into the following sections: exhibitions, motion picture stills; intermediate chemicals; explosives; man-made fiber research and production; Rayon, Nylon; Orlon, Dacron, Lycra; cellulose sponges; photo products; packaging films; plastics; synthetic rubbers; fabrics and finishes; pigments and dyes; metals and alloys; coolants; automotive products; agricultural chemicals; toxicological studies; atomic energy; and research facilities.

Most of the photographs date from 1930 to 1960. There are some original negatives.

## Accessions #68.25, 69.11, 69.23, 71.MSS.775

**PUBLIC RELATIONS DEPARTMENT MISCELLANEOUS PICTURE FILES**

402 items

c. 1900–1950

Part I—Photographs gathered for the 150th Anniversary of the Du Pont Company, including portraits of executives, chemists, inventors, and miscellaneous employees. Also includes views of Repauno, Eastern Laboratory, the Experimental Station, miscellaneous plants, and carving Mt. Rushmore with explosives.

Part II—Miscellaneous photographs, including portrait of cellophane superintendants (1944), rayon dresses, fabrikoid tableclothes, Wilmington views, copy negatives of pictures from various sources for PR use, and du Pont family photographs.

## Accessions #70.58, 76.354, 82.216

**RAYON DEPARTMENT COLLECTION**

247 items

1920–1953

Photographs of rayon and early nylon research, manufacturing process, and plants. Also includes group portrait of executives (c. 1950) and views of Ducilo S. A. Producto de Rayon Berazategui, Argentina (1937).

See also 72.341.

## Accessions #71.MSS.833, 72.266, 72.373, 76.309, D91–1

**REPAUNO (N.J.) PLANT AND EASTERN LABORATORY COLLECTION**

466 items

c. 1895–1955

Photographs of Repauno, New Jersey dynamite works buildings, machinery, employees, housing, aftermaths of explosions, and Eastern Laboratory research facilities and staff.

See also 68.1.G54, 69.11, 69.142, 70.221, 72.341 (Box 6), 73.328, 77.240, and 82.300.

## Accession 72.436

**FRANK G. TALLMAN COLLECTION**

175 items

c. 1865–1930

Photographs, mostly family and personal, of Du Pont Company Vice-President Frank G. Tallman (1860–1938), including some relating to Warner and Tallman families. Also includes views of Du Pont Company executives.

In addition to the preceding checklist, the following subjects are contained in various small accessions too numerous to list here. Detailed finding aids are available in the Pictorial Collections and Audio-Visual Services Department.

    I.    **POWDER YARDS ON THE BRANDYWINE AND SURROUNDING AREAS**
1890–1950
389 items

    II.    **DU PONT COMPANY EXECUTIVES, EXECUTIVE GROUPS, BOARD OF DIRECTORS, EMPLOYEES, AND EMPLOYEE GROUPS.**
1900–1970
237 items

    III.    **EXPERIMENTAL STATION, WILMINGTON, DELAWARE**
1908–1952
48 items

    IV.    **DU PONT BUILDING, WILMINGTON, DELAWARE**
1905–1950
23 items

    V.    **MISCELLANEOUS EXPLOSIVES PLANTS AND MAGAZINES**
1899–1955
279 items

    VI.    **MISCELLANEOUS NON-EXPLOSIVES PLANTS AND SITES**
1901–1965
270 items

    VII.    **COMPANIES ABSORBED BY THE DU PONT COMPANY**
1875–1920
158 items

    VIII.    **MISCELLANEOUS AND UNIDENTIFIED PLANTS**
1890–1965
246 items